Finding, Preparing, and Supporting School Leaders

Finding, Preparing, and Supporting School Leaders

Critical Issues, Useful Solutions

Edited by
Sharon Conley and
Bruce S. Cooper

ROWMAN & LITTLEFIELD EDUCATION
A division of
ROWMAN & LITTLEFIELD PUBLISHERS, INC.
Lanham • *New York* • *Toronto* • *Plymouth, UK*

Published by Rowman & Littlefield Education
A division of Rowman & Littlefield Publishers, Inc.
A wholly owned subsidiary of The Rowman & Littlefield Publishing Group, Inc.
4501 Forbes Boulevard, Suite 200, Lanham, Maryland 20706
http://www.rowmaneducation.com

Estover Road,
Plymouth PL6 7PY,
United Kingdom

Copyright © 2011 by Sharon Conley and Bruce S. Cooper

All rights reserved. No part of this book may be reproduced in any form or by any electronic or mechanical means, including information storage and retrieval systems, without written permission from the publisher, except by a reviewer who may quote passages in a review.

British Library Cataloguing in Publication Information Available

Library of Congress Cataloging-in-Publication Data

Finding, preparing, and supporting school leaders : critical issues, useful solutions / edited by Sharon Conley and Bruce S. Cooper.
   p. cm.
  Includes bibliographical references and index.
  ISBN 978-1-60709-837-9 (cloth : alk. paper) — ISBN 978-1-60709-838-6 (pbk. : alk. paper) — ISBN 978-1-60709-839-3 (electronic : alk. paper)
  1. School administrators—Recruiting—United States. 2. School administrators—Training of—United States. 3. Educational leadership—United States. I. Conley, Sharon C. II. Cooper, Bruce S.
  LB2831.82.F56 2011
  371.2'011—dc22
                                                             2010041790

∞™ The paper used in this publication meets the minimum requirements of American National Standard for Information Sciences—Permanence of Paper for Printed Library Materials, ANSI/NISO Z39.48-1992.

Printed in the United States of America

Contents

1. From Administrator Recruiting to Retention — 1
   Bruce S. Cooper and Sharon Conley

2. Teaching and Preparing School Leaders — 11
   Margaret Terry Orr and Diana G. Pounder

3. Teaching Principals to Be Master Teachers, Again — 41
   Roberta Trachtman and Bruce S. Cooper

4. Midcareer Teachers and Principals — 65
   William H. Marinell

5. New Principal Isolation and Efficacy — 89
   Scott C. Bauer and S. David Brazer

6. Assistant Superintendents Moving to the Superintendency — 113
   David F. Leach and Bruce S. Cooper

7. Superintendent Leadership — 137
   George J. Petersen

Epilogue: Thoughts for the Future — 155
Naftaly S. Glasman and Lynnette D. Glasman

About the Contributors — 161

Chapter One

From Administrator Recruiting to Retention

Bruce S. Cooper and Sharon Conley

School leaders, teachers, staff—and parents—are all concerned about getting and keeping the best leaders for their schools. This book tells them how: what to do (and not to do) to accomplish these goals. In particular, the book characterizes the qualities of administrator recruitment, socialization, career development, and approaches to school management for preparing school leaders and supporting them in the education profession.

The book looks at the features of administrator preparation, professional development practices, administrator-teacher relationships, use of resources, changing work environments, and new models of school administration that are promising in preparing the best leaders for U.S. schools. As Berliner (2007) emphasized, schools are essentially human enterprises, and the cultivation and retention of critical personnel who staff them are paramount.

In exploring leader preparation and socialization, Bolman and Deal (2002) provide the example of Jaime Rodriguez, a rookie principal. During a disastrous first faculty meeting, Rodriguez's remarks about his vision for a child-centered school are interrupted by an experienced teacher's objection ("Shouldn't you get to know this school and how we do things before you preach about how we should teach?") (p. 17). Fortunately, Rodriguez is helped by veteran educator Brenda Connors to sort through the confusing events of his new job. Through subsequent mentoring from Principal Connors, Jaime gets a better handle on what is happening and renews his commitment to school leadership.

Many educators will be familiar with this example, especially in schools led by new administrators or an inexperienced administrative team. But who is responsible for ensuring positive school management, human development and capacity building, and change? How are school improvement and change accomplished? In what ways can the leadership of both administrators and teachers be nourished? How can educators stimulate growth in a system that examines and takes into account school culture, community, and educational experience?

To address these questions, this book takes a broad, eclectic approach, bringing together a range of scholars examining leadership preparation and the administrator life cycle. As Crow (1990) asks:

> What motivates principals to carry out [their] weighty responsibilities? Is it less important to understand the incentives of instructional leaders than to understand what motivates teachers? If we can identify those features of the role that entice administrators to perform these responsibilities, district and state policy makers will be in a better position to develop incentives that retain and recruit effective instructional leaders. (p. 38)

Site and district leaders occupy difficult and complex jobs, and the trainees for and the incumbents in these jobs deserve closer attention and help. Universities and other job preparation programs need a deeper understanding of what works. Therefore, this book brings together some of the latest research and practices to sustain and improve U.S. schools. As we know from years of research, leadership is important to figuring out what's working or not working, and thus what needs changing, and how best to proceed.

The book is an essential resource for future leaders, education faculty in universities, professional associations, school district leaders, board members, and others interested in preparing and providing in-service education for the 200,000-plus leaders of American schools and school systems.

What we can learn from the perspectives and examples presented in this book will help in several ways: (1) to improve the nature of professional preparation, support, and mentoring needed to sustain our leaders; (2) to focus planning of in-service activities for working school administrators at all levels; (3) to help leaders throughout their careers do a better job; and (4) importantly, to keep the flow of new leaders coming, as they go from teaching, to transitioning to site leadership positions, to ascending to the central office, to considering the superintendency and remaining there. And researchers of the professions and of school leadership development will want to read this book, as it has implications for human and professional development, now and into the future.

THE PROBLEM

School leaders, at the school site and district levels, have never had an easy job. With dwindling funds and resources, coupled with tougher state and federal standards, and fatigue from more regulations and testing, many school administrators are giving up—or crashing and leaving their posts. Richard O. Carlson (1969) discovered years ago that organizations in need of change are more likely to look outside their borders for new talent, while schools and districts that are working well may wish to promote from within. Based on data from a sample of superintendents in the Northwest, Carlson identified differences between what he termed career bound and place bound superintendents.

Career bound superintendents assigned primary importance to the career as superintendent versus living in a particular geographic location, often had held multiple superintendencies (and were called "hoppers"), and had made the decision to become a superintendent at an early age. Place bound superintendents, in contrast, often had a history in the school district in which the decision to become a superintendent was made, and had established a set of social relations and loyalties (and rivalries).

But in focusing on these career and work orientations, Carlson doesn't examine in depth the organizational career development and qualities of good recruiting, reviewing, responding, renewing, and rewarding that could lead to better levels of retention—the Six R's (Mulvey & Cooper, 2009) of good professional development and support.

In Mulvey and Cooper's (2009) recent book, the Six R's were applied to teacher careers: leading from Recruitment to Retention, *with the critical Four R's in between*: Reviewing, Renewing, Responding, and Rewarding; presently, the Six R's are being applied to leadership support as we seek to find, build, and hold on to new leaders in our schools and districts (see Figure 1.1).

Today, new school leaders may be asked to administer the more challenging schools, such as those identified as chronically low performing in urban, suburban, and rural locations. In New York City, for example, Mulvey and

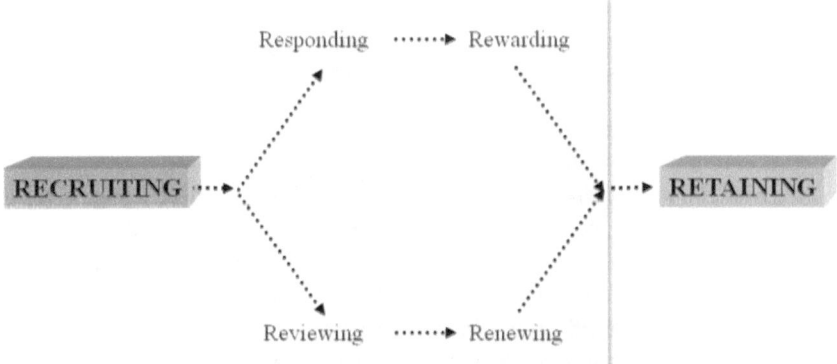

Figure 1.1. Six R's of New Teacher Retention: Conceptual Framework for Retaining Quality Personnel

Cooper (2009) described the difficulties of low-performing schools, staffed in part by teachers placed on "fast tracks" for certification.

Principals, who often had a hand in hiring these personnel and who were also charged with their orientation and socialization, faced a high turnover of these new teachers early in the principals' tenures, even when the number of teacher recruits was initially encouraging. Although principals seemed likely to recruit new education graduates, the majority of fast-track program teachers were often either change-of-career (midcareer) candidates or older personnel reentering the workplace (Mulvey & Cooper, 2009).

These challenges were faced by principals amid their striving to meet academic standards driven by No Child Left Behind (NCLB), as well as responding to the needs of increasingly diversified student populations, demonstrating a commitment to equity for all students.

Recognizing the complicated problems faced by school and district leaders, this book begins with Mulvey and Cooper's (2009) Six R model to examine the process of finding, encouraging, and retaining quality leaders at the school and district levels. The steps in the process are (1) *Recruiting and Preparing* quality new administrators and (2) *Responding* to their needs; (3) *Reviewing* them in ways that are helpful; (4) *Rewarding and Recognizing* administrators who have grown in their work; (5) *Renewing* their spirit and skills to build stronger administrator confidence and understanding; and thus (6) *Retaining* quality administrators in schools.

Describing career growth and development among teachers, Guskey (2000) outlined several professional development activities that were critical to school improvement and personnel adjustment and longevity.

> The kind of organization support needed for a workshop or seminar, for example, may be quite different from what is essential for study groups or *peer [teacher and administrator] coaching*. That difference is why discussions of organization support and change are so vital in the earliest stages of any professional development endeavor. (Guskey, cited in Mulvey & Cooper, 2009)

So the process of keeping new administrators charged with providing such critical organizational supports follows these six steps:

Step 1—*Recruiting and Preparing* new school and district leaders: With shortages in many districts, schools and districts need to pay attention to finding quality administrators, providing them with "realistic" job previews (Wanous, 1973) and ensuring a match between the administrative job, the school, and the leader. Step 6—*Retaining* these administrators: We need to track the careers of administrators, from preparation to advancement through the administrative ranks, finding ways of helping administrators be successful with teachers at different stages of their careers.

The four intervening steps are important, going in between Recruiting and Retaining, and helping to ensure that administrators are adjusting to their work and remain in the leadership profession.

Step 2—*Responding*: This step involves the role of the district and school leadership in focusing on and responding to the needs of education leaders as they take on and are socialized into their posts and includes ideas related to Job Satisfaction (feeling the job generally meets expectations) and Growth Satisfaction (feeling the job is an outlet for further growth and development) (Conley, Shaw, & Glasman, 2007; Hackman & Oldham, 1980).

Step 3—*Reviewing and Understanding* leaders' needs and growth regularly are regarded as critical to new school improvement (Crow, 2007). Feedback is the key: not critical or threatening; when it comes from administrative superiors and/or mentors showing understanding and being helpful.

Reviews can be directed toward improving various roles of school leadership such as instructional, transformational, and managerial/strategic (Leithwood & Duke, cited in Glasman & Heck, 2003) or strengthening leaders' compliance with the school community's expectations (Glasman & Heck, 2003). Yet as the role of school leaders becomes more complex, so too does the difficulty of reviewing and understanding leaders' needs.

For school principals, structural reforms such as charter schooling, decentralizing, and school choice may blend traditional roles in very specific patterns for each leader (Glasman & Heck, 2003; Smylie & Crowson, 1993). Reviews should include discussions about individual performance as well as opportunities for improved work design and further career development, that is, features of principals' jobs that focus on immediate opportunities to work on "meaningful" tasks or which career paths might provide a more continuous sense of career progression over time.

Finally, Step 4—*Rewarding and Recognizing* have been shown to be important for administrators throughout their careers (Marshall & Kasten, 1994). Distinct periods of time in the career trajectories of site leaders include trainee, intern, assistant principal, novice principal, and experienced principal (Glasman & Glasman, 2007). Administrators may focus on different undertakings at different times. For example, newcomers seek opportunities to exercise autonomous decision making and to facilitate collaborative work with others, whereas experienced leaders seek to serve as exemplary models "while working on conflict" and developing "a greater love of people, learning, and teaching" (Glasman & Glasman, 2007, pp. 136, 154).

In addition to financial compensation, providing leaders much-needed recognition for their accomplishments; helping them to communicate what they are doing to other administrators (colleagues and superiors in the administrative hierarchy); and reaching out to teachers, parents, and their communities are key steps in sustaining and retaining them (Crowson & Morris, 1985).

Additional nonmonetary rewards include "variety and challenges" in job tasks and having the ability to contribute to and maintain contact with students and staff (Crow, 1990). While it is possible that an administrator might move on, retire, or take another job, staying on the job—and succeeding—are still the goals of most leaders and their schools. To ensure that administrators won't necessarily quit, give up, or find another position, *Retaining* (Step 6) continued leadership requires a *Renewal* (Step 5) of spirit, knowledge, and growth—giving feedback and more time for reflection (Bolman & Deal, 2008; Collinson & Cook, 2007).

BOOK OVERVIEW

Most states require both principals and superintendents to be licensed, based on experience and graduate credits, and usually expect candidates for the school and district qualification to spend time in internships related to these jobs. This book addresses the move toward standardization of the background and education of administrators who are recruited to schools, based on the Interstate School Leaders Licensure Consortium's (ISLLC) standards.

Professional organizations like the National Policy Board for Educational Administration (NPBEA) and the University Council for Educational Administration (UCEA) play a key role in maintaining standards and improved training for the next generation of leaders—and professors who teach the graduate courses—and who do the research in the field of school leadership.

Beyond university preparation, the book also examines the processes of adjusting to and being well socialized into the position—and recognizing and understanding changing resources and roles as well as difficulties encountered in these increasingly political, exposed positions under federal, state, and local pressures.

Taking a longer view, we examine leaders' key allies within schools and systems and what associations and associates are important to helping them to keep positive work attitudes, learn new techniques, and survive on the job. Self-efficacy beliefs and social support are perceived as important—and playing the political survival games may come to the forefront. The career ladders are critical, if slippery, at times, and fewer educators are risking it.

Another issue, commonly called the leadership "pipeline," is the pathway into the principalship (usually "flowing" from the classroom to the assistant principal's office to the top job in the school) and the stairways to the top job in the district: the superintendency. If leaders are unwilling to leave the security of the number two job for the top one, where will the next generation of school leaders really come from? Already school systems in major cities have hired lawyers, businesspeople, even political figures, since assistant superintendents do not always look to move up, and may prefer the security and protection of the deputy positions.

The book takes a look at assistant superintendents, a group often ignored in the research. How effective and satisfying is the position, and what are the key interactions and relationships that affect these leaders and their decisions to seek promotion—or not? What is the organizational culture that can hurt a career as a superintendent (the executive school leader) and what can be done to make the roadways safer and better?

THE CHAPTERS

In this chapter, the Six R Model was a loose guide for organizing our thoughts for the rest of the chapters.

In Chapter 2, "Teaching and Preparing School Leaders," Margaret Terry Orr and Diana G. Pounder provide an overview of important factors in preparation programs that contribute to effective learning and career outcomes for administrator candidates. The chapter integrates policy, research, and case studies of programs to specify recommendations for quality leader preparation programs.

In Chapter 3, "Teaching Principals to Be Master Teachers, Again," Roberta Trachtman and Bruce S. Cooper apply an evaluation methodology to examine key factors influencing novice teacher retention and the role principals play in the selection, induction, and long-term development of teachers. Salient findings focus on the culture, structures, and resources for teacher learning, and opportunities for leadership and decision-making. Particular attention is paid to urban settings, owing to their unique challenge: how do principals support and retain quality teachers who are often in short supply?

In Chapter 4, "Midcareer Teachers and Principals," William H. Marinell explores what leaders need to know about the utilization of teachers who enter the profession after having worked outside of education. Such fast-track teachers bring a wealth of knowledge to their schools that can help administrators accomplish school objectives of improving student learning. The chapter considers how administrators might both draw new resources into their schools and capitalize on what already exists within their organizations.

In Chapter 5, "New Principal Isolation and Efficacy," Scott C. Bauer and S. David Brazer use quantitative methods to examine the role that isolation plays in new principals' sense of self-efficacy, that is, their beliefs about the ability to be successful in achieving school goals. Based on data from a survey of first-year principals in one state, the chapter finds that the role stress factors of ambiguity, and to a lesser extent, role overload, need to be addressed for new principals to feel efficacious in their work. In addition, social support structures, which reduce the degree of isolation felt by new principals, appear promising in improving leaders' emotional states and enhancing self-efficacy.

In Chapter 6, "Assistant Superintendents Moving to the Superintendency," David F. Leach and Bruce S. Cooper present data and findings from a regional survey of assistant superintendents of schools about their background, roles, work, and outcomes (e.g., satisfaction, efficacy, and future ambitions for promotion). Key findings from their quantitative analysis are that assistants who reach their fifties are much less likely to seek the top post, meaning that preparation and training must start earlier if assistants are going to rise to the top positions.

In Chapter 7, "Superintendent Leadership," George J. Petersen examines several major problems faced by executive leaders of schools in their professional lives. This chapter pays particular attention to the needs of school leaders and what we can learn from their experiences to prepare the next generation. The chapter also explores the purpose and importance of professional development for district superintendents.

Finally, in the Epilogue, "Thoughts for the Future," Naftaly S. Glasman provides a summation of the book's chapters, identifies pertinent themes, and offers additional insights about what can be done to get and keep better (and more) school leaders in these challenging times.

The book, then, offers a wide and detailed perspective on renewing educational leaders as they deal with the many challenges faced in American public schools. Beginning with a chapter on leadership preparation and concluding with thoughts about accountability in schools, the various chapters offer contemporary views on aspects of preparing school administrators throughout their life cycle. As such, they provide needed insight into what should and must be done to grow the best leaders for U.S. schools.

REFERENCES

Berliner, D. C. (2007). Foreword. In A. B. Danzig, K. M. Borman, B. A. Jones, & W. F. Wright (Eds.), *Learner-centered leadership: Research, policy, and practice* (pp. xi–xiv). Mahwah, NJ: Lawrence Erlbaum.

Bolman, L. G., & Deal, T. E. (2002). *Reframing the path to school leadership: A guide for teachers and principals*. Thousand Oaks, CA: Corwin.

Bolman, L. G., & Deal, T. E. (2008). *Reframing organizations: Artistry, choice, and leadership*. San Francisco: Jossey-Bass.

Carlson, R. O. (1969). *Career and place bound school superintendents: Some psychological differences. A project report.* Eugene, OR: Eugene Center for Advanced Study of Educational Administration.

Collinson, V., & Cook, T. F. (2007). *Organizational learning: Improving learning, teaching and leading in schools and school systems.* Thousand Oaks, CA: Sage.

Conley, S., Shaw, S., & Glasman, N. (2007). Correlates of job and professional satisfaction among secondary school administrators. *Journal of School Leadership, 17*(1), 54–88.

Crow, G. M. (1990). Perceived career incentives of suburban elementary school principals. *Journal of Educational Administration, 28*(1), 38–52.

Crow, G. M. (2007). The professional and organizational socialization of new English headteachers in school reform contexts. *Educational Management Administration and Leadership, 35*(1), 51–71.

Crowson, R. L. & Morris, V. C. (1985). Administrative control in large-city school systems: An investigation in Chicago. *Educational Administration Quarterly, 21*(4), 51–70.

Eckman, E. W. (2004). Similarities and differences in role conflict, role commitment, and job satisfaction for female and male high school principals. *Educational Administration Quarterly, 40*(3), 366–387.

Glasman, N. S., & Glasman, L. D. (2007). *The expert school leader: Accelerating accountability.* Lanham, MD: Rowman & Littlefield.

Glasman, N. S., & Heck, R. H. (2003). Principal evaluation in the United States. In T. Kellaghan and D. L. Stufflebeam (Eds.), *International handbook of educational evaluation* (pp. 630–656). Dordrecht, Holland: Kluwer Academic Publishers.

Guskey, T. (2000). *Evaluating professional development.* Thousand Oaks, CA: Corwin Press.

Hackman, J. R., & Oldham, G. R. (1980). *Work redesign.* Reading, MA: Addison-Wesley.

Hoy, A. W., & Hoy, W. K. (2006). *Instructional leadership: A research-based guide to learning in schools.* (2nd edition). Boston: Allyn and Bacon.

Leithwood, K., & Duke, D. (1999). A century's quest to understand school leadership. In J. Murphy & K. Seashore-Louis (Eds.), *Handbook of research on educational administration* (2nd ed.) (pp. 45–72). San Francisco: Jossey-Bass.

Marshall, C., & Kasten, K. L. (1994). *The administrative career: A casebook on entry, equity, and endurance.* Thousand Oaks, CA: Corwin Press.

Mulvey, J. D., & Cooper, B. S. (2009). *Getting and keeping new teachers: Six essential steps from recruitment to retention.* Lanham, MD: Rowman & Littlefield.

Smylie, M., & Crowson, R. (1993). Principal assessment under restructured governance. *Peabody Journal of Education, 68*(2), 64–84.

Wanous, J. P. (1973). Effects of a realistic job preview on job acceptance, job attitudes, and job survival. *Journal of Applied Psychology, 58*(3), 327–332.

Chapter Two

Teaching and Preparing School Leaders

Margaret Terry Orr and Diana G. Pounder

This chapter examines the important qualities of preparation programs that contribute to effective learning and career outcomes for aspiring school and district leader candidates. The results are drawn from professional guidelines and comparative research on exemplary leadership preparation programs to provide a framework of critical program features and specific examples drawn from effective leadership preparation programs. Recommendations for future research on educational leadership preparation are included.

BACKGROUND

Demand is growing for educational leadership preparation that enables graduates to advance quickly and efficaciously into initial school and district leader positions (Frye, O'Neill, & Bottoms, 2006; Wallace Foundation, 2003). The twin problems of existing and anticipated shortages in highly qualified leaders and the demands for leaders who can improve and sustain high levels of student performance in schools have brought a new and sharper focus to the quality and effectiveness of university-based leadership preparation.

While the number of currently certified candidates exceeds the number of school building leadership positions within and across states (Educational Research Service [ERS], 2000; ERS, National Association of Elementary School Principals, & National Association of Secondary School Principals, 1998; Gates, Ringel, Santibanez, Ross, & Chung, 2003), analyses of labor market conditions reveal shortage conditions and areas.

First, the labor pool of aspiring leaders erodes quickly, as candidates lose interest if they do not advance within a few years of becoming licensed. Second, some certified candidates have conflicting concerns about leadership positions, anticipating professional benefits as well as difficult or stressful working conditions (Farkas, Johnson, Duffett, & Foleno, 2001; Pounder & Merrill, 2001).

Third, the leadership job market is changing, with the addition of more diverse leadership positions than just principals and superintendents (e.g., curriculum specialists, teacher leaders/facilitators/coaches, professional development specialists, business officers, human resource administrators), requiring more leaders; and finally some types of positions and district locations are more difficult to fill than others (Browne-Ferrigno & Muth, 2009; Papa, Lankford, & Wyckoff, 2002; Ringel, Gates, Chung, Brown, & Ghosh-Dastidar, 2004). Taken together, these conditions show a need for high-quality leadership preparation to develop candidates who are ready for a wide variety of leadership roles, responsibilities, and challenges.

Increasingly, districts view leadership quality and its development as essential to school improvement and effectiveness, particularly for schools that struggle to make academic gains. Among strategies that districts, particularly urban districts, are now using to improve school quality is to expect principals to focus on instructional leadership, to distribute leadership responsibilities to others, to use data to guide instructional decisions, and to support teacher professional development (Togneri & Anderson, 2003).

In turn, to strengthen leader quality, some districts are now developing their own leadership preparation programs (as competition or a complement to university-based programs) or engaging in partnership with local universities to tailor preparation to their context (Orr, King, & La Pointe, 2009 draft).

Some evidence, as will be reviewed below, suggests that investment in leadership preparation program improvement and adoption of innovative approaches pay off, particularly when supplemented with grant or foundation funding for full-time internships. Additional research reviewed below suggests that graduates of programs with these quality features have more positive views of the principalship and are more interested in a leadership career. Thus, investing in preparation program quality has a positive effect on the aspiring leader labor pool as well as on the quality of leadership practiced by new leaders.

What, then, are the features of highly effective leadership preparation programs? And which program features have greatest influence on graduates' career and learning outcomes, with corresponding benefits for the schools they eventually lead?

ABOUT THIS CHAPTER

This chapter draws together policy, research, and case studies on leadership preparation program features to highlight converging findings on key features and essential dimensions of effective preparation program attributes. It shows the policy recommendations and research reviews that converge in common recommendations for quality program features. Available research on the relationship between program features and outcomes underscores those features that are most critical for candidates' learning, career outcomes, and leadership work. These features are illustrated with case examples drawn from research on exemplary programs.

STANDARDS FOR AND RESEARCH EVIDENCE OF PROGRAM QUALITY FEATURES

Policy and research represent two primary sources that define program quality features and guidance for program improvement. Analyses of policy and research recommendations and conclusions serve as a framework for this chapter.

Policy Guidelines

Policy expectations for leadership preparation program quality exist in national accrediting bodies, state regulations, and professional standards. Weak and varied expectations for school leaders, coupled with the recognition of the centrality of leadership to school effectiveness, led to the development of national leadership standards to frame public expectations and guide preparation, licensure, and candidate and program evaluation (Council of Chief State School Officers, 1996). These standards, known as the Interstate School Leaders Licensure Consortium (ISLLC) standards, were eventually adopted by almost every state as the basis for leadership preparation expectations (Toye, Blank, Sanders, & Williams, 2007).

In 2002, the National Policy Board for Educational Administration (NPBEA) adopted the ISLLC standards for preparation program accreditation. In turn, its specialized professional association, the Educational Leadership Constituent Council (ELCC), developed guidelines for programs to implement these standards and provide evidence of program effectiveness (NPBEA, 2002).[1] Table 2.1 summarizes the program feature expectations outlined in these guidelines.

The guidelines focused largely on program content, based on the leadership standards for expected candidate knowledge and skills to promote the success

Table 2.1 National Professional Standards for Leadership Preparation Programs

Quality program features	ELCC program implementation standards (National Policy Board for Educational Administration, 2002)	UCEA program guidelines (1991, revised 1998) (www.ucea.org)	SREB guidelines for quality university-based leadership preparation (Bottoms et al., 2003; Southern Regional Education Board, 2006)
Program theory	—	Conceptually coherent	Design the program to emphasize school-based learning
Standards based	Delineates six standards, based on the national ISLLC standards	Conceptually coherent and clearly aligned with quality leadership standards	Refers to standards as the basis for course content, assignments, and other learning experiences for competency development
Candidate recruitment and selection	—	Have systematic, written recruitment and admission plans that rely on multiple sources of evidence and show deliberate efforts to attract applicants who demonstrate leadership potential with particular attention given to increasing diversity within the program	Identify and select candidates with demonstrated leadership ability, knowledge of curriculum and instruction, and proven high performance Candidates are selected jointly by university and district partners using a shared criteria
Content	Standards-based content based on expected leader knowledge and skills (i.e., develop, articulate, and implement a vision; exhibit instructional leadership; manage organization, operations, and	Identify, develop, and promote relevant knowledge focused on the essential problems of schooling, leadership, and administrative practice Program content and design is informed by current scholarship on the essential problems of schooling, leadership, and administrative practice and should make use of research-based best practices in leadership preparation	Emphasis on knowledge and skills for improving schools and raising student achievement, and on the principal's responsibilities in improving curriculum, instruction and student achievement Focus on authentic problems and the development of leadership competencies Customized to district needs

Table 2.1 National Professional Standards for Leadership Preparation Programs

Content *Continued...*	resources; facilitate family and community collaboration; behave fairly and ethically; understand, respond to, and influence education context)	The content should address problems of practice including leadership for student learning and diversity	Collaboratively developed by university and district staff Coherently organized
Active instruction	--	The instructional processes of the preparation program should be based on adult learning principles	Create learning experiences in which candidates apply research-based knowledge to solve real school problems and focus on the core functions of schools Enable competency mastery Assignments and projects that are school-based and that address real problems pertaining to student achievement
Quality internship	Internship offers significant opportunities to apply knowledge and develop leadership skills; is substantial, sustained, standards-based, planned and supervised by the university and school district; and earns credits	Include concentrated periods of study and supervised clinical practice in settings that give leadership candidates an opportunity to work with diverse groups of students and teachers	Well-planned and supported field experiences that are integrated with coursework throughout the program, are mentored by master leaders, and enable candidates to practice their skills with reflection Reflects a continuum of practice for competency mastery Provides performance feedback and coaching by faculty or other supervisors Includes mentor planning

Table 2.1 National Professional Standards for Leadership Preparation Programs

Cohort structure and other program supports	—	Program is customized for students based on their current positions and leadership opportunities Provides supports and conditions for program completion, such as tuition, release time, mentoring, and materials
Program organization	—	Team-teaching of course-related modules Time, resources and staffing to develop a new curriculum Solicit state waivers for certification issues that are barriers to leadership preparation
Mentoring and advisement	—	—
Career support	—	Develop and maintain systematic efforts to assist all students in professional placement and career advancement
Postpreparation programs	—	Participate in the development, delivery, and evaluation of systematic professional development programs for educational leaders, in cooperation with appropriate professional associations and other educational and social agencies
Candidate and program evaluation	Standards-based assessments of candidates' content knowledge, skills, and leadership effectiveness	Engage in ongoing programmatic evaluation and enhancement	Rigorous evaluation of participants' mastery of essential competencies and program quality and effectiveness Uses reliable measures of performance and a clearly defined exit criteria

Table 2.1 National Professional Standards for Leadership Preparation Programs

Candidate and program evaluation *Continued* . . .		Includes on-the-job performance assessments
		Faculty support to conduct ongoing evaluation on the effectiveness of the program in preparing leaders who can increase student learning and improve schools
		Include faculty work in schools as part of tenure and promotion requirements
Knowledgeable and competent faculty	Dedicated, knowledgeable faculty	Involve a critical mass of full-time tenure-track faculty members (typically five or more) whose appointments are in the department in which educational leaders are educated and who exhibit excellence in scholarship, teaching, and service in educational leadership. A majority of educational leadership coursework must be taught by these full-time faculty.
	Expectations that faculty will engage in research and professional service and have educational leadership experience	
	Expectation that faculty will use assessment data to improve candidate and program performance	
Faculty professional development	—	Offer regular professional development for program faculty to enhance their skills in leadership preparation, research methods, and other content areas
		Provide faculty and others with broad, research-based knowledge
		Support faculty in developing and field-testing leadership training modules that address real problems of principals and involve real learning experiences in schools
		Faculty time to conduct research in schools

Table 2.1 National Professional Standards for Leadership Preparation Programs

Collaboration	—	Engage in collaborative relationships with other universities, school districts, professional associations, and other appropriate agencies to inform program content, promote diversity within the preparation program and the field, and generate sites for clinical study, field residency, and applied research	University/district partnerships for principal preparation that is formal, definitive and institutionalized Universities work with school districts on candidate selection
Advisory board or committee	—	Use an advisory board of educational leadership stakeholders and involve leadership practitioners in program planning, teaching, and field internships	Create an advisory board with business, education, state, and university representatives to meet regularly and design the program

of all students. However, the ELCC standards provide few specific program structure or process guidelines, with three exceptions. These are the inclusion of extensive guidelines in defining the attributes of a quality internship, candidate assessment requirements, and guidelines for faculty assignment and responsibility in program management.

A second set of program standards was developed by the University Council on Educational Administration (UCEA) in 1991 and revised in 1998, as shown in Table 2.1. The University Council for Educational Administration is a professional association that is a consortium of primarily doctoral-granting higher education institutions with a demonstrated commitment to the preparation and practice of educational leaders. Full member institutions must both be doctoral granting and provide evidence that they satisfy (or are making significant progress toward satisfying) UCEA's program standards. These standards go farther than other guidelines by focusing both on the quality of the program and the roles and actions of the faculty and institution in service to quality leadership preparation.

A third set of program standards, as shown in Table 2.1, was developed and is promoted by the Southern Regional Educational Board (SREB), particularly among institutions in its 16 member states for university-based program redesign (Bottoms, O'Neill, Fry, & Hill, 2003; Frye et al., 2006; SREB, 2002). These guidelines are tightly organized around learning and competency development for leadership to improve student learning and thus focus content and field experiences on knowledge of the core functions of schools and the ability to solve real school problems.

The three sets of program standards are most similar in emphasizing the use of:

- Leadership standards to frame the program, align preparatory experiences, and provide coherence
- An intensive internship experience that enables leadership skill development and authentic leadership experiences, under the supervision of university and practicing administrators
- Program evaluation to monitor candidate progress and improve program quality
- High-quality faculty

They differ in several key areas, however. First, only the ELCC guidelines stress a specific set of standards—the ISLLC standards—as the basis for program content and candidate competencies. Second, the ELCC guidelines, aside from emphasizing standards, provide limited guidance on candidate selection criteria, instructional strategies, and use of organizational supports.

In contrast, the UCEA and SREB guidelines outline recommended criteria for candidate selection (including demonstrated leadership potential). Both emphasize the importance of developing relevant knowledge and focusing on problems of practice.

UCEA stresses research-based best practices in leadership and attention to diversity, while SREB emphasizes tying principal practices to student achievement gains and customizing program content to district needs. UCEA stresses the use of adult learning theory in instructional approaches, while SREB singles out application of program knowledge to real school problems and core school functions. Both UCEA and SREB focus on the institutional conditions of university-based programs, emphasizing faculty professional development, collaboration with districts, and the use of advisory boards with broad representation to inform program design and delivery. Finally, only the UCEA guidelines give attention to candidates' career support and postpreparation programs.

Research on Quality Leader Preparation

Extensive reviews of research on exemplary leadership preparation programs and quality program features (Davis, Darling-Hammond, Meyerson, & La Pointe, 2005; Jackson & Kelley, 2002; McCarthy, 1999; Orr, 2006; Young, Crow, Ogawa, & Murphy, 2009) point to similar attributes of quality features. This work is complemented by case study analyses of exemplary programs (Darling-Hammond, Meyerson, La Pointe, & Orr, 2009; U. S. Department of Education, 2004) and Murphy and Orr's (2009) recommendations for essential program features—based on their research and evaluation experience in the field (Murphy, 2006; Orr, 2009). Taken together, this research, as summarized in Table 2.2, points to a common set of quality program features. These are:

- Has a well-defined theory of leadership for school improvement that frames and integrates the program features around a shared vision, philosophy, or set of principles
- Is standards based
- Recruits and selects candidates based on leadership potential
- Has a coherent curriculum that addresses effective instructional leadership and school improvement
- Uses adult learning theory, developmental learning principles, or active learning strategies to facilitate learning and connect coursework and fieldwork
- Offers quality internships and other field-based experiences that provide intensive, developmental opportunities to apply leadership knowledge and skills under the guidance of experienced mentors or supervisors

Table 2.2 Recommended Quality Features of Educational Leadership Preparation Programs Based on Research Reviews and Case Study Analyses

Quality program features	(Jackson & Kelley, 2002)	(Orr, 2006)	(U.S. Department of Education, 2004)	(Darling-Hammond, Meyerson, La Pointe, & Orr, 2009)	(Murphy & Orr, 2009, Spring)
Program theory	Focus Use of a visioning/revisioning process that fosters program coherence	Reframing organizing principles to create clearly defined visions and articulated fundamental principles	Guiding vision of powerful school leadership	A philosophy and curriculum that emphasize instructional leadership	Based on a well-developed and articulated set of foundational principles about leadership and its preparation that frame program content and experiences
Standards based	Often developed around the ISLLC standards	Uses national standards	Uses local, state, and national leadership standards	A comprehensive and coherent curriculum aligned with state and professional standards, in particular ISSLC standards, which emphasize instruction leadership	Based on the ISLLC and ELCC standards for candidates and programs, respectively
Candidate recruitment and selection	Application process and selection criteria to reflect leadership potential	Student selection	Selectivity, based on prior experiences and dispositions for school leadership (including passion, commitment, and self-awareness),	Vigorous, targeted recruitment and selection to seek out expert teachers with leadership potential	Recruitment Has a proactive plan to secure desired candidates Encourages candidates to apply or be nominated based on their potential leadership qualities and demonstrated instructional effectiveness

Table 2.2 Recommended Quality Features of Educational Leadership Preparation Programs Based on Research Reviews and Case Study Analyses

				Selection
Candidate recruitment and selection *Continued* . . .	and uses a comprehensive screening process			Assesses and values the extent to which candidates demonstrate: intent to be school leaders; prior leadership experience; excellence in teaching; commitment to and experience working as an advocate for children and families; commitment to and alignment with the foundational principles of the program Selects candidates who meet eligibility and admissions requirements of the institution; Is selective in admissions
Content	Clear, well-defined curriculum focus reflecting agreement on the relevant knowledge base for new leaders	Curriculum and coursework that are coherently organized	Standards-based curriculum	A comprehensive and coherent curriculum . . . that emphasizes instruction leadership A philosophy and curriculum that emphasize instructional leadership and school improvement	Aligns with the foundational principles of the program Is constructed on the ISLLC leadership standards Reflects research on effective leadership and school improvement Reflects best practice in curriculum design Integrates technology effectively Is integrated into a coherent scope and sequence Is intellectually challenging Is scaffolded on practice

Table 2.2 Recommended Quality Features of Educational Leadership Preparation Programs Based on Research Reviews and Case Study Analyses

Content *Continued...*				Highlights skills and qualities needed to lead schools and school improvement effectively
Active instruction	Design learning around fieldwork Use team teaching or other instructional strategies	Active learning strategies rooted in adult learning; create more dynamic learning experiences in both coursework and field experiences	Use adult learning theory to facilitate learning	Active, student-centered instruction that integrates theory and practice and stimulates reflection	Reflects deep understanding of developmental learning principles Features active instructional practices to evoke transformative learning Makes appropriate use of technology Emphasizes the development of higher-order cognitive processes through applied learning experiences
Quality internship	Lengthy internships (600 plus hours)	Internship and field experiences	Internship with expert mentors Mentor selection and training often included	Well-designed and supervised administrative internships that allow candidates to engage in leadership responsibilities for substantial periods of time under the tutelage of expert veterans	Clinical Work Aligns with the foundational principles of the program Is aligned with the ISLLC leadership standards Anchors the program (i.e., is integral part of the program) Is woven throughout the program (i.e., not confined to internship) Features authentic leadership work (not passive activities and observations)

Table 2.2 Recommended Quality Features of Educational Leadership Preparation Programs Based on Research Reviews and Case Study Analyses

Quality internship *Continued...*			Is aligned with the school year and the time-flow of leadership responsibilities Is tightly linked to classroom learning experiences **Internship** Is designed around the quality dimensions of clinical work above Meets the ELCC standards for an effective building-level internship Is developmental, with increasing responsibilities progressing to independent leadership responsibilities Is supervised by a highly qualified school leader and a faculty advisor Is of considerable length and intensity
Cohort structure and other supports	Cohort based; use of structures to sequence curriculum developmentally; foster strong connections among students and with faculty for meaningful discussions about leadership	Use of cohort structures for pedagogical purposes	Begin the program with an intensive and highly focused induction process Develop a supportive cohort structure	Social and professional support in the form of a cohort structure and formalized mentoring and advising by expert principals	Promotes supportive learning structures for students (e.g., cohort design) Links students with excellent mentors

Table 2.2 Recommended Quality Features of Educational Leadership Preparation Programs Based on Research Reviews and Case Study Analyses

Cohort structure and other supports *Continued...*	Career supports	
	Limit enrollments to 20 to 25 candidates	
Program organization	Structure and delivery (e.g., length, credits, and sequence of courses and fieldwork) to capitalize on fieldwork and school cycles	Makes available and integrates technology appropriately
		Fosters the development of a community of practice among students and faculty
		Ensures timely program completion
		Ensures that learning experiences occur during the school day (not on the margins of the teacher's day)
Candidate assessment and program evaluation	Candidate and program assessments used for candidate and program development	**Candidate assessment**
		Is based on the ISLLC standards
		Is based on the program's foundational principles
	Use of national standards and accreditation to evaluate their impact on graduates and on the schools their graduates lead	Reflects best practice in measurement
		Is scaffolded on authentic conditions of leadership and problems of practice
	Candidate performance assessment	Is more than a collection of course grades
		Program evaluation
	Program performance assessment	Is an important and well planned dimension of the program
		Uses best practice of program evaluation and assessment
	Substantial use of feedback and assessment by peers, faculty, and the candidates themselves	

Table 2.2 Recommended Quality Features of Educational Leadership Preparation Programs Based on Research Reviews and Case Study Analyses

Candidate assessment and program evaluation *Continued* . . .		Measures institutional performance across a variety of desired outcomes Provides performance feedback for changing the program Ensures that evaluation data are directed to strengthening the program
Knowledgeable and competent faculty	Staffing Faculty who are knowledgeable in their subject areas, including both university professors and experienced practitioners	Demonstrates dedication and commitment to the vision, mission, and guiding principles of the program Maintains close contact with schools Includes a balance of theoretical and practical experiences Includes a sufficient number of full-time and part-time faculty Demonstrates recent highly effective leadership experience in schools and districts Includes educators from partner districts Works as a community of professional practice
Faculty professional development		Engages in regular professional development experiences to strengthen knowledge and skills

Table 2.2 Recommended Quality Features of Educational Leadership Preparation Programs Based on Research Reviews and Case Study Analyses

Collaboration	Significant faculty and practicing administrator collaboration Strong district collaboration	District-university collaborations as a means of significant innovation in leadership preparation	Program is based on a district-university partnership	Ensures that practitioner partners are meaningfully involved in all core program elements (e.g., recruitment and selection, instruction, program evaluation, and so forth) Draws on local districts for current issues, problems, and challenges facing educational leaders Works collaboratively to develop authentic and meaningful clinical and internship experiences, with high-quality mentoring

- Provides cohort structures or other supports to enhance learning and foster strong student and faculty connections
- Uses assessments for candidate and program feedback and continuous improvement that are tied to the program vision and objectives
- Engages knowledgeable faculty with relevant field-based experiences
- Engages in collaborations or partnerships with local districts in program development and delivery

These reviews of research and case study analyses focused less on program organization, such as the length and timing of programs, and on faculty development and institutional factors addressed in the standards review in Table 2.1.

One review, by Jackson and Kelley (2002), offers a conceptual design on the relationship among the program features that is reflected as well in the reviews and case study analyses of others. What this design reinforces, as shown in Figure 2.1, is the synergistic relationship between students, faculty, and content, as facilitated by program structures, processes, and strategies. The authors argue that the tighter and more coherent the interplay among these, the more powerful the learning and leadership development. Such coherence is also stressed in the research reviews and case study analyses.

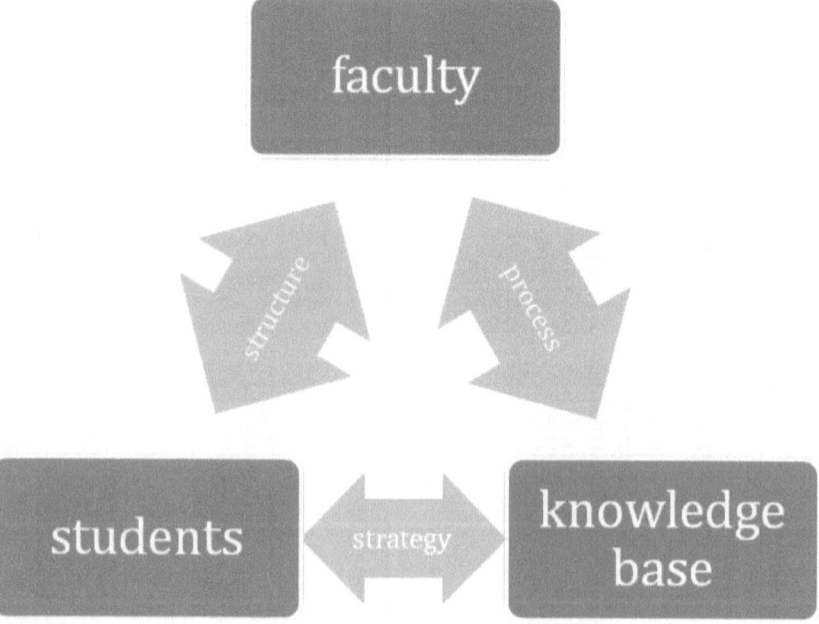

Figure 2.1. Conceptual Design of Leadership Preparation Program Features

Research on Leadership Preparation Outcomes

A small body of research has investigated the relationship between leadership preparation program quality features and graduate and school leader outcomes, the results of which are shown in Table 2.3. Two studies investigated the relationship between quality program features and initial graduate outcomes: what graduates learned about leadership, their beliefs about the principalship as a career, and their actual career advancement. The studies were modeled on the theory of planned behavior that asserts that career intentions are strongly predictive of subsequent career advancement and are influenced by individuals' perceived efficacy and beliefs about the position (Ajzen, 1991), and on other related research on beliefs about the principalship and career aspirations (Pounder & Merrill, 2001).

In one study, Orr and Barber (2007) compared the outcomes for graduates of two university-district partnership programs (both designed to include many of the innovative features identified above) with outcomes for graduates of a conventional program (with few such features). They found that three program features—supportive program structures (such as accessibility and scheduling convenience); a comprehensive and standards-based curriculum; and broader, more intensive internships—were significantly but differentially related to three types of outcomes: self-assessed leadership knowledge and skills, leadership career intentions, and actual career advancement.

Similarly, Orr (2010) examined how differences in 17 programs' incorporation of these innovative features and overall program redesign to meet national and state standards were associated with graduate learning and career outcomes. The 17 programs varied most on measures of three types of program features: program challenge and coherence, use of active student-centered instructional practices, and internship length and quality. How graduates rated their preparation program features was significantly related to how much they learned about instructional and organizational leadership. The length and quality of internships, however, were uniquely associated with graduates' career intentions and subsequent career advancement.

In addition, two other studies investigated the relationship between preparation program features and candidates' outcomes as school leaders. Leithwood et al. (1996) documented eleven innovative graduate-level leadership preparation programs that were redesigned through a Danforth Foundation grant initiative and correspondingly surveyed teachers who worked in schools led by program graduates. The authors found that the programs' innovative use of several features—instructional strategies, cohort membership,

Table 2.3 Program Features That Are Significantly Associated with Graduate Outcomes

Quality program features	(Leithwood, Jantzi, Coffin, & Wilson, 1996)	(Orr & Barber, 2007)	(Orr, 2010 [forthcoming])	(Orr & Orphanos, 2010 [forthcoming])
Recruitment and selection	X—active recruitment and careful selection	—	—	—
Challenging, reflective program	—	—	X—extent to which the program was comprehensive and coherent, challenging, intellectually stimulating and fostered reflection	NS
Program content	NS	—	X—leading learning content focus	X—Emphasizing instructional leadership, integrated theory and practice, knowledgeable faculty, and having a strong orientation to the principalship as a career
Instruction	X—active and reflective learning strategies, such as projects, problem-based learning, and reflective seminars	—	X—active learning instruction such as problem-based, case-based, and action research learning	NS
Internship	X—nature and quality of internship and the leadership work done	X—quality internship features	X—quality internship (based on the six ELCC characteristics)	X—having responsibilities for leading, facilitating and making decisions typical of an educational leader; being able to develop an educational leader's perspective on school improvement, and having an excellent learning experience for becoming a principal

Table 2.3 Program Features That Are Significantly Associated with Graduate Outcomes

Quality program features	(Leithwood, Jantzi, Coffin, & Wilson, 1996)	(Orr & Barber, 2007)	(Orr, 2010 [forthcoming])	(Orr & Orphanos, 2010 [forthcoming])
Mentoring	NS	--	--	--
Cohort structure and other supports	X—focused on the quality of positive student relationships	NS	X—being part of a cohort X—positive student relationships	NS
Structure	X—timing, sequencing, and other supportive structures	NS	X—supportive organizational structures	NS
Faculty	--	--	X—knowledgeable, competent faculty	(as included with a measure of program quality)
Evaluation	X—opportunities for self-assessment and program evaluation	--	--	NS
Partnership	X—collaborative, tailored program planning	--	X—whether the program is based on a district-university partnership	NS

X = statistically significant relationship exists
NS = the relationship was tested and not found to be statistically significant
-- the relationship was not tested

and program content—was most predictive of teachers' positive perceptions of principals' leadership effectiveness (such as in setting direction, developing staff, fostering a positive school culture, and focusing on curriculum and instruction).

Orr and Orphanos (2010), using survey research conducted in 2005 as part of Stanford University's study of exemplary leadership preparation for the Wallace Foundation, compared 65 principals who had graduated from one of four selected exemplary leadership preparation programs with a national comparison sample of 111 principals. Using structural equation modeling (SEM), they investigated the influence of exemplary leadership preparation on principals.

Their findings showed that principals' participation in an exemplary leadership preparation program was positively and significantly associated with the extent to which they learned about instructional and organizational leadership and how frequently they engaged in these leadership practices in their schools. Stronger relationships existed when measures of preparation program quality and internship quality were taken into account.

The most significant features of quality internships included having responsibilities for leading, facilitating, and making decisions typical of an educational leader; being able to develop an educational leader's perspective on school improvement; and having an excellent learning experience for becoming a principal. The most significant features of program quality included program content that emphasized instructional leadership, integrated theory and practice, knowledgeable faculty, and having a strong orientation to the principalship as a career.

Moreover, for these principals, frequent use of effective leadership practices was positively associated with the extent of school improvement progress, and school effectiveness climate, although the extent of challenging problems had a moderating influence on the degree of school improvement progress. Taken together, exemplary leadership preparation had a positive, but mediated influence on variations in school improvement progress and school effectiveness climate; the relationship is even stronger when including preparation program and internship quality measures (Orr & Orphanos, 2010, forthcoming).

An analysis of common findings of the four studies in Table 2.3 reveals the strongest convergence of findings around the influence of a high-quality internship (using the ELCC definitions of quality) on graduate outcomes and their practices as school leaders. Other findings that existed in two or three studies showed the positive association of program content that emphasizes instructional leadership, the use of active, reflective instructional strategies, and supportive structures, including cohort membership.

Only one study found positive significant findings related to whether the program was part of a district-university partnership; used active recruiting and careful screening; used collaborative planning; had a challenging and reflective program focus; had knowledgeable, competent faculty; and gave opportunities for program evaluation. The absence of significant findings in the other three studies was related primarily to the lack of measurement rather than null associations.

Other studies are beginning to use measures of leadership preparation in their investigation of leadership effectiveness. For example, Tschannen-Moran and Gareis (2005), in their study of 558 principals, found that principals' perceived quality and utility of leadership preparation significantly contributed to their sense of leadership self-efficacy. Combined, these results underscore that the quality of how candidates are prepared relates to their subsequent leadership practices and work.

QUALITY FEATURES IN ACTION

Much of the research on leadership preparation has been case study based (Murphy & Vriesenga, 2006; Orr, 2009), serving as a resource on how programs can design and implement specific features and practices. Only in a few cases, however, has such research been validated by external reviewers or evaluation evidence. Darling-Hammond and others' (2009) research provides strong evidence on the effectiveness of four exemplary programs.

We draw on these programs to illustrate three critical program features underscored by the analyses of policy guidelines, research reviews, and research studies. Specifically, we will use these exemplary programs to illustrate (1) coherent program focus and organization; (2) active learning instructional approach; and (3) a broad and intensive, quality internship.

Coherent, Focused Program

Delta University's educational leadership preparation program, located in rural Mississippi, is based on a clearly articulated program philosophy and an aim of developing school leaders who are capable of transforming the poor, rural schools in its region. This 14-month Master of Education program is designed as an interdisciplinary set of weekly seminars and internship experiences, through which leadership theory and concepts are integrated around issues, events, and problems experienced in practice. Candidate knowledge and skills are assessed through portfolio assignments and reflection activities, rather than course-specific assignments.

Active Learning-Centered Instruction

Bank Street College's Principals' Institute, an 18-month, 36-credit master's degree program, infuses active learning-centered instruction in the program's design, coursework, and fieldwork. When partnering with local districts (such as Region 1, as described in the 2009 Darling-Hammond et al. report), the program is integrated and aligned with local priorities, to enhance program content and learning opportunities. Candidates are enrolled as a cohort, taking the same courses together through the program. They are assigned to smaller conference groups of 6 to 8 candidates each, facilitated by an advisor who is an experienced school or district leader, a process known as the college's advisement model.

As part of this model, conference groups meet regularly throughout the program for facilitated discussions to connect theory to practice, engage in problem solving around internship-related experiences, and focus on the candidates' development as new school leaders. The internship is organized as a developmental progression, ranging from conducting a study of the school site to taking on increasingly independent work.

An inquiry approach is infused across the courses, and applied inquiry and research is a final program course enabling candidates to investigate a problem of practice in their own setting. Finally, journaling and reflection is incorporated into coursework and is shared weekly between each candidate and his or her advisor to deepen their leadership development and problem solving.

Quality Internship

An example of a quality internship experience was the University of San Diego's Educational Leadership Development Academy (ELDA) program. It supported a full-time, yearlong paid internship that assigned candidates to work with experienced principals who were specifically selected for their expertise, instructional improvement effectiveness, and mentoring skills. The internships were designed to be developmental, offering gradually increasing responsibility and independence, and focused primarily on instructional responsibilities. Mentor principals and their candidates met regularly to discuss approaches to and solutions for problems that arose in the schools.

The candidate and mentor principal selection and assignment processes were facilitated by the program's strong partnership with the San Diego Unified School District. Funding for paid internships was made possible by a private foundation grant. When the program ended, the district continued the model after the participants had completed the academy. The district was able to adapt the model for a smaller number of candidates by placing them in assistant principal positions.

CONCLUSIONS AND RECOMMENDATIONS

In the past decade or two, perhaps largely motivated by concerns about school effectiveness, more policy and research have emerged that focus on leader preparation quality and outcomes. This chapter summarized and compared some of the more salient policy developments and research findings to triangulate those program features that hold greatest promise for effective leader preparation. The results show strong convergence among policy guidelines, best practices research, and research relating program features and outcomes. Some of the more well-substantiated of these "effective leader preparation program features" may be synthesized as follows:

- Standards-based program content that has a strong emphasis on leadership for learning or instructional leadership
- Program coherence that reaches across program curriculum, field experiences, and instructional processes
- Candidate selection that prioritizes demonstrated leadership potential and instructional effectiveness
- Authentic, active-learning instructional processes that utilize adult learning principles
- In-depth internship and clinical experiences that closely link to program standards
- Cohort-based structure or other supportive learning structures that tighten relationships among program candidates and faculty and that enhance professional socialization and induction
- Ongoing and rigorous performance assessment that enhances candidate and program improvement
- A critical mass of faculty that reflects a balance of theoretical and practical knowledge and who participate actively in teaching, research, and university-school-professional association collaboration

Less researchable, but equally important as stressed in the guidelines and some of the best practices research, is attention to the program management and institutional support that is necessary for high-quality leadership preparation. These include: faculty professional development, regular use of program evaluation, and input from the field on program content, quality, and effectiveness. Most critical among the organizational features is the importance of collaboration or partnership with local districts, both to inform content and keep programs relevant, and to share in the responsibility of recruiting and selecting candidates, teaching, and supporting internships.

Given these advances in our understanding of leader preparation quality, broader distribution of these findings is needed to better inform policy makers, aspiring leaders, the general public, and even some leader preparation program faculty. In particular, this information needs to be shared in publication venues that reach lay audiences. For too long, because of insufficient knowledge about educator preparation quality, our profession was able to rebut public criticism with little more than anecdotal evidence. However, armed with greater systematic evidence, we can more clearly educate policy makers, aspiring leaders in search of high-quality career preparation, university faculty, and others about the characteristics and value of well-designed and well-supported leader preparation programs. We no longer must plead ignorance about "what works" effectively to prepare school leaders.

Nonetheless, we have more empirical work to do . . . particularly to uncover and verify the complex array of candidate characteristics and preparation and development experiences that enhance leaders' capacity to improve school conditions and student learning outcomes. At present, very little of the work done on leader preparation effects has included independent assessments of school leaders' effectiveness—such as assessments by subordinates (i.e., teachers), assessments by superordinates (i.e., district leaders or others), or other independent indicators of effectiveness around student learning. However, recently developed leader assessment tools can facilitate valid and reliable measurement of school leader effectiveness.

These assessment tools include the UCEA School Leadership Preparation and Practice Survey and its parallel teacher survey (www.ucea.org/evaluation-tools) used to assess graduates and their school leadership, and the VAL-ED Principal Assessment Instrument (www.discoveryeducation.com/products/assessment/val_ed.cfm), used for principal performance evaluation. This additional evidence is likely to strengthen the depth and complexity of our understanding of leader preparation, development, and leader effectiveness.

In sum, the knowledge base on leader preparation has expanded considerably in the last decade or more. Greater distribution of this enhanced knowledge is needed along with continuing efforts to strengthen the empirical evidence of leader preparation effects.

NOTE

1. The ELCC is the recognized specialized professional association to review educational leadership programs for NCATE accreditation. NCATE's Specialty Areas Study Board approves the standards. The professional association that develops the guidelines for implementing standards, in this case the ELCC, is a constituent member of NCATE. www.ncate.org/public/standards.asp?ch=4

REFERENCES

Ajzen, I. (1991). The theory of planned behavior. *Organizational Behavior and Human Decision Processes, 50,* 179–211.

Bottoms, G., O'Neill, K., Fry, B., & Hill, D. (2003). *Good principals are the key to successful schools: Six strategies to prepare more good principals.* Atlanta, GA: Southern Regional Education Board.

Browne-Ferrigno, T., & Muth, R. (2009). Candidates in educational leadership graduate programs. In M. D. Young, G. Crow, J. Murphy & R. Ogawa (Eds.), *Handbook of research on the education of school leaders* (pp. 195–244). New York: Routledge.

Council of Chief State School Officers. (1996). *Interstate School Leaders Licensure Consortium: Standards for School Leaders.* Washington, DC: Author.

Darling-Hammond, L., Meyerson, D., La Pointe, M. M., & Orr, M. T. (2009). *Preparing principals for a changing world.* San Francisco: Jossey-Bass.

Davis, S., Darling-Hammond, L., Meyerson, D., & La Pointe, M. (2005). *Review of research. School leadership study. Developing successful principals.* Palo Alto, CA: Stanford University, Stanford Educational Leadership Institute.

Educational Research Service. (2000). *The principal, keystone of a high-achieving school: Attracting and keeping the leaders we need.* Arlington, VA: Author.

Educational Research Service, National Association of Elementary School Principals, & National Association of Secondary School Principals. (1998). *Is there a shortage of qualified candidates for openings in the principalship? An exploratory study.* Arlington, VA: Author.

Farkas, S., Johnson, J., Duffett, A., & Foleno, T. (2001). *Trying to stay ahead of the game: Superintendents and principals talk about school leadership.* New York: Public Agenda.

Frye, B., O'Neill, K., & Bottoms, G. (2006). *Schools can't wait: Accelerating the redesign of university principal preparation programs.* Atlanta: Southern Regional Educational Board.

Gates, S. M., Ringel, J. S., Santibanez, L., Ross, K., & Chung, C. H. (2003). *Who is leading our schools? An overview of school administrators and their careers.* Santa Monica, CA: Rand Corporation.

Jackson, B. L., & Kelley, C. (2002). Exceptional and innovative programs in educational leadership. *Educational Administration Quarterly, 38*(2), 192–212.

Leithwood, K., Jantzi, D., Coffin, G., & Wilson, P. (1996). Preparing school leaders: What works? *Journal of School Leadership, 6*(3), 316–342.

McCarthy, M. M. (1999). The evolution of educational leadership preparation programs. In J. Murphy & K. S. Louis (Eds.), *Handbook of research on educational administration: A project of the American Educational Research Association* (pp. 119–139). San Francisco: Jossey-Bass Publishers.

Murphy, J. (2006). *Preparing school leaders.* Lanham, MD: Rowman & Littlefield Education.

Murphy, J., & Orr, M. T. (2009, Spring). Industry standards for preparation programs in educational leadership. *LTEL-SIG Newsletter, 17*(1), 9–11.

Murphy, J., & Vriesenga, M. (2006). Research on school leadership preparation in the United States: an analysis. *School Leadership & Management, 26*(2), 183.

National Policy Board for Educational Administration. (2002). *Instructions to implement standards for advanced programs in educational leadership for principals, superintendents, curriculum directors and supervisors.* Arlington, VA: Author.

Orr, M. T. (2006). Mapping innovation in leadership preparation in our nation's schools of education. *Phi Delta Kappan, 87*(7), 492–499.

Orr, M. T. (2009). Program evaluation in leadership preparation and related fields. In M. D. Young & G. Crow (Eds.), *Handbook of research on the education of school leaders.* New York: Routledge.

Orr, M. T. (2010, forthcoming). Assessing educational leadership preparation: A comparison of programs' quality features and graduates' learning and career outcomes. *Educational Administration Quarterly.*

Orr, M. T., & Barber, M. E. (2007). Collaborative leadership preparation: A comparative study of innovative programs and practices. *Journal of School Leadership, 16*(6), 709–739.

Orr, M. T., King, C., & La Pointe, M. M. (2009 draft). *Districts developing leaders: Eight districts' lessons on strategy, program approach and organization to improve the quality of leaders for local schools.* Report prepared for The Wallace Foundation. Newton, MA: EDC.

Orr, M. T., & Orphanos, S. (2010, forthcoming). How preparation impacts school leaders and their school improvement: Comparing exemplary and conventionally prepared principals. *Educational Administration Quarterly.*

Papa, F., Lankford, H., & Wyckoff, J. (2002). *The attributes and career paths of principals: Implications for improving policy.* Albany, NY: University of Albany, SUNY.

Pounder, D. G., & Merrill, R. J. (2001). Job desirability of the high school principalship: A job choice theory perspective. *Educational Administration Quarterly, 37*(1), 22–57.

Ringel, J. S., Gates, S. M., Chung, C. H., Brown, A., & Ghosh-Dastidar, B. (2004). *Career paths of school administrators in Illinois.* Santa Monica, CA: Rand Corporation.

Southern Regional Education Board. (2002). *Are SREB states making progress? Tapping, preparing and licensing school leaders who can influence student achievement.* Atlanta, GA: Southern Regional Educational Board.

Southern Regional Education Board. (2006). *Schools can't wait: Accelerating the redesign of university principal preparation programs.* Atlanta, GA: author.

Togneri, W., & Anderson, S. E. (2003). *Beyond islands of excellence: What districts can do to improve instruction and achievement in all schools.* Washington, D.C.: Learning First Alliance.

Toye, C., Blank, R., Sanders, N. M., & Williams, A. (2007). *Key state education policies on P-12 Education: 2006. Results of a 50 state survey.* Washington, D.C.: Council of Chief State School Officers.

Tschannen-Moran, M., & Gareis, C. R. (2005). Cultivating principals' sense of efficacy: Supports that matter. Annual convention of the University Council of Educational Administration. Nashville, TN.

U.S. Department of Education. (2004). *Innovations in Education: Innovative pathways to school leadership*. Washington, D.C.: U.S. Department of Education, Office of Innovation and Improvement.

Wallace Foundation. (2003). *Beyond the pipeline: Getting the principals we need, where they are needed most*. New York: Wallace Foundation.

Young, M. D., Crow, G., Ogawa, R., & Murphy, J. (2009). *The handbook of research on leadership preparation*. New York: Routledge.

Chapter Three

Teaching Principals to Be Master Teachers, Again

Roberta Trachtman and Bruce S. Cooper

School principals at one time were "master teachers," "head teachers," and even in some places, "headmasters." But no longer. With their school responsibilities for operations, finances, testing, and conferencing many days with parents, community leaders, teacher unions—not to mention the district meetings with the superintendent and central office staff—principals hardly have time to visit their teachers' classrooms, consult with them about their lessons, and help them adjust to the mounting pressures of having their students make Adequate Yearly Progress (AYP) under state and federal laws, such as No Child Left Behind (NCLB).

New principals, in mastering their jobs, need to know, use, and support best practices in classroom teaching—which remain the key activity in education (Brown & Wynn, 2007). And universities that train and serve these building leaders should be stepping up to prepare their principal candidates to be active *teacher leaders*. In fact, since courses like "Becoming Teacher Leaders" are rarely offered as part of the programs for principals' preparation and master's programs, we see what happens in our schools. Some new teachers find a home and get the mentoring and coaching they need from fellow teachers. Others become isolated and lost, and often abandon teaching after a year or two. Lack of teacher support for new teachers is a critical problem; and we have some suggestions for school principal preparation programs—and in-service workshops—to help new principals to once again become "principal teachers" and not just building managers.

These recommendations are based on studies commissioned by the New Jersey Consortium for Urban Education (NJCUE), an association dedicated to preparing teachers to work in some of the nation's toughest urban school districts—by using a fast track, new "pathway to certification" in the state of New Jersey. This state is the most urbanized, the highest spending, and the most diverse in the United States—an excellent place to test the processes of finding, preparing, and keeping new teachers, and the role of school principals in the process.

In this chapter, we explore implications of principals' roles as "master teachers"—for the university graduate programs that prepare and recertify these school leaders, and the districts that retrain and support them. The outcomes are clear: that is, the ability to find and retain quality new teachers, who are in short supply. The needs are also obvious: the preparation, training, and support of school building leaders who have time to concentrate on, and the skills to assist, teachers in their classrooms, and with their students.

THE FAST TRACK PROGRAMS

The shortage of urban teachers has become widespread, and a number of "fast track" programs such as Teach for America (TFA), the New York Teaching Fellows Program, and the New Jersey Consortium for Urban Education (NJCUE) have responded. The New Jersey version, the NJCUE, concentrated on two teacher licenses, K-5 general and K-8 special educators, using this approach as the basis for assessing the needs and possible actions of school leaders who could help prepare and support teachers in their work in the classrooms. The NJCUE had the following goals for teachers:

- Complete 33 graduate credits, tuition free, to meet requirements for Dual State Certification
- Accumulate graduate credits that might apply toward a Master of Arts in Teaching degree
- Earn a $2,000 summer stipend during student teaching (note the short experience, summers only)
- Receive intensive mentoring during the summer and the first year of teaching
- Participate in ongoing teaching and curriculum seminars and workshops
- Finally, receive peer coaching during the second and third years of the Program

Interestingly, in its final year of five years of operation, NJCUE re-aimed its focus, piloting a professional development program for principals and in those schools that had hired NJCUE novice teachers.

It is this group that we are targeting in this chapter, exploring the lessons learned that might be applied to the overall preparation and training of school building leaders. The principles and activities guiding this program and our analysis include (1) Differentiated Professional Development for new teachers, in concert with other district efforts; (2) Team-Based Structures for all teacher support; and (3) Restructured and Reallocated Time.

Mentoring as Key

A review of recent research (e.g., Wong, 2004) suggests three approaches for developing and retaining new teachers: (1) *mentoring*, the assistance of one individual through the support of another; (2) *induction*, the array of structures, strategies, and resources to recruit, select, orient, and develop new teachers; and (3) *integration*, which is the broadest approach schoolwide—with the development of new teachers who are tied to and integrated into the development of the school as a learning organization. Whereas induction often includes mentoring, it also integrates additional school-based professionals and learning opportunities for new teachers.

Definitions and Uses

Across disciplines and professions, mentoring involves guiding and facilitating less-experienced colleagues' efforts toward individual or professional goals and their integration into work cultures (Black & Puckett, 1996; Gallacher, 1997). Henry, Stockdate, Hall, and Deniston (1994) define mentoring as "a caring and supportive interpersonal relationship between an experienced, more knowledgeable practitioner (mentor) and a less experienced, less knowledgeable individual (protégé or mentee), in which the protégé receives career-related and personal benefits" (as cited in McCormick & Brennan, 2001, p. 132). Gallacher (1997) further elaborates that mentoring not only transmits practical, concrete knowledge to the mentee, but also positive attitudes, beliefs, and values.

Principals who might "match" mentors with mentees and/or facilitate teacher induction, collaboration, rewards, and support in other ways might consider the following aspects of mentoring: teacher mentor quality, mentoring program structure, mentoring versus induction, and schoolwide professional learning communities.

Teacher Mentor Quality

As research documents the strong influence mentors can have on a teaching mentee's teaching and development (Bennett & Carré, 1993; Colbert & Wolff, 1992; Houston, McDavid, & Marshall, 1990), experts caution that the existence and degree of influence vary in quality. Indeed, the quality and selection of a mentor appear critical elements in the mentoring relationship and a key factor in the effectiveness of a mentoring program (Feiman-Nemser & Parker, 1993; Little, 1990).

As the trend toward mentoring in teacher education and development gains wider acceptance in formalized structures, studies outlined the characteristics of effective mentors within schools. Gibb and Welch's (1998) interviews with mentees in Utah revealed the importance of attitudes and interpersonal skills that supported the mentoring of teaching skills. Mentors rated as flexible, nonthreatening, enthusiastic, and open-minded were those who possessed strong communication and listening skills: for example, trustworthiness and confidentiality were considered most effective by mentees.

Researchers and practitioners alike identify effective mentors as master professionals, actively engaged in their fields with an appreciation for environmental and contextual factors that affect their protégés' work. Ragins, Cotton, and Miller (2000) argue that mentoring may be marginal or significant, depending on the type of mentor, the relationship, and program design. Successful mentoring relationships are frequently constructed on mentor-mentee dyads with similarities both personal and professional (Huling-Austin, 1990; Little, 1990; Odell & Ferraro, 1992). For example, mentor and mentee might be of the same gender and race and teach in the same certification area, at the same grade level and school. More generally, effective mentors work under the same conditions, both curricular and environmental, and in the same field/subject area as their mentees.

Mentoring Program Structure

Particular characteristics of a mentoring program support the effectiveness of the mentor-mentee relationship. Along with mentor criteria and training, Feiman-Nemser and Parker (1993) consider formal expectations and mentor-mentee working conditions as critical variables to success. Experts differentiate between assessment and evaluation and urge that mentoring programs specifically state their purpose (e.g., Feiman-Nemser & Parker, 1993). Mentoring programs should match the needs of mentors and mentees; otherwise, perceived benefits are considered minimal (Little, 1990). Time allocated to the work of mentoring indicates the importance of the mentor-mentee relationship to participants and other vested parties (Colbert & Wolff, 1992; Huling-Austin, 1992; Little, 1990). Mentors and mentees must have time to work together without compromising their other professional responsibilities (Little, 1990).

Mentoring versus Induction

Over the past two decades, teacher mentoring programs have become the dominant form of teacher induction. Analysts and practitioners often use the terms *teacher induction* and *teacher mentoring* interchangeably (Fideler & Haselkorn, 1999). In his work, however, Wong (2004) drew significant distinctions between the two approaches. Induction is a comprehensive, coherent, and sustained professional development process organized by a school district to train, support, and retain new teachers and help them develop into *lifelong learners.*

Mentoring, in contrast, is a set of actions performed by a single person whose basic purpose is to help the new teacher *survive*; generally, the mentor focuses on the novice's immediate, pressing needs, rather than the development of the teacher as a professional educator. Similarly, Britton, Paine, Raizen, and Pimm (2003) defined effective induction programs as having a focus on career-long professional learning through collaboration. Most importantly, these researchers indicated that the function of the induction phase was to engender a sense of group identity and integrate new teachers into the school community.

Schoolwide Professional Learning Communities

While teacher mentoring remains the most typical form of new teacher support, a growing research literature points to other, potentially more compelling approaches. Others, like Schlager, Fusco, Koch, Crawford, and Phillips (2003), posited that since new teachers' needs were so varied and immediate, the appropriate combination of expertise, experience, and cultural background was unlikely to reside in one mentor who would be available when needed. Similarly, in her four-state large-scale study, Kardos (2004) found a strong, positive correlation between new teachers' ongoing professional interaction with experienced colleagues and job satisfaction. She concluded that new teachers' preferences for such collegial work had implications for novices' career decisions.

EVALUATION METHODOLOGY

As Cummins recently articulated (2009, p. 385), "Ethnographic and case study data contribute to theory (and knowledge generation) primarily by establishing phenomena that require explanation." To that end, we sought to generate knowledge about teacher preparation and retention and principals' roles by capturing the experiences of New Jersey alternate route-prepared teachers and the principals with whom they worked. In the study described below, we first collected field data from principals and teachers, formed hypotheses to account for these initial understandings, and tested these hypotheses against additional data collected in a follow-up study.

While we describe the follow-up studies elsewhere in detail (Allenwood Company, 2008), we note here that we used Cummins's earlier work (1999) to define the second and third follow-up studies; with those additional data, we began to formulate theories related to the role of school leaders in supporting and retaining novice teachers.

To investigate the key factors influencing novice teacher retention, we asked six principals if we could meet for an hour with their first-, second-, and third-year teachers to learn more about their experiences as novices (some fourth-year NJCUE graduates participated as well). We conducted focus groups with 40 novice teachers in the spring of 2008; approximately 40% of the teachers in the focus groups were NJCUE graduates, most of whom were special education teachers. Given our interest in understanding the induction process and how it relates to teacher retention, and what principals can do to improve the process, we focused the discussion on the teachers' areas of growth and to what they attributed their development, their experiences as new teachers, and their perceived strengths and weaknesses.

Analyses

Data from the focus groups were analyzed using an iterative process of interpretation, triangulation, and evidence testing. The early data analyses prompted new questions, new inquiries, and new understandings. We examined our initial findings from these 40 novices in relation to the second round of data that we collected in Study 2, described below.

To develop a deeper understanding about why NJCUE novices continue to teach, and to expand our group of key informants, we developed a telephone protocol for interviewing as many program graduates as we could find. At that time, NJCUE Cohort I teachers were completing their fifth year of teaching; those in Cohort II were finishing their fourth year; Cohort III their third year; and Cohort IV their second year. Given our interest in understanding why novices stay in teaching and administrator-teacher relationships, the interview questions focused on the kinds of support teachers receive, their relations with colleagues and administrators, and the broader working conditions at their schools.

Interview Response Rates and Participants

The original sampling strategy, based on a target overall sample size of 50 teachers, called for a random sampling of teachers from each of the four NJCUE cohorts in numbers proportional to the cohort sizes with a minimum of 10 teachers per cohort.

However, this stratified sampling model was modified as the process unfolded. We discovered that the contact information for earlier cohorts was more likely to be out of date than for the later cohorts. Even when the information seemed to be valid, the response rate to the initial contact email, which explained how important their participation was to the NJCUE evaluation and requested that the teachers schedule an appointment for an interview, was much lower for earlier cohorts compared to later ones. Despite repeated email requests for interviews to an expanded number of Cohort I and II teachers, we were still unable to interview very many of them. Of the 46 teachers interviewed, 5 were from Cohort I, 7 from Cohort II, 11 from Cohort III, and 23 from Cohort IV.

First Contacts, Real Help

We learned that new teachers are most vulnerable during their first months on the job. Principals need to know when to act—and earlier is better than too late.

As one teacher explained:

> Basically, when I started here, you were thrown under the bus! There's an orientation but it's just from the district, and it's not very helpful. It's not by grade level—for Pre-K to high school meeting all in one room. It was outdated, too broad, and generic. It's not designed for a particular school.

And, as another concurred and added:

> Yes, I got a handbook at the beginning of the year, but it doesn't tell us *anything* about the real school you're in. I needed someone to tell me exactly what kind of kids I was going to have and to talk about the general problems in the school.

So it is obvious that the problems begin even before the new teachers arrive on the job. In addition to the unwelcome and "lost" feelings engendered by the lack of specific orientation activities, teachers were concerned about not being briefed on school policies and procedures, worrying that this lack of information could have led to serious problems. One teacher provided a compelling example:

> We had a big fire drill and there was this procedure: pull your kid out of the line and alert the principal right away. You know, my kid has wandered off; like maybe the kid was in the bathroom, but I didn't know about that and neither did my assistant. So when did they decide to do that to one of my kids?—when I'm out and she's by herself with 17 kids. She almost had a heart attack. She sees Katie is missing and she's like, "Oh my god." They finally told her, "Oh, we took Katie because we want to make sure you're counting."

One summarized the sentiments of many teachers when she said:

> I feel like it's a form of almost hazing. It's like you come in, nobody tells you anything, and you've got to learn it yourself. The fact is, if you would have sat down with any one of us and said, "tell me the real story," we'd tell you the real story. Your life would be 1000% better. You would have been a much better teacher just for knowing how things work. But no one tells you that. And everyone knows that's the way it is, but that's the way it goes, sink or swim.

And yet, some responded positively, like the teacher who said: "Our principal sends us to a lot of good workshops. We're a small school and we have a lot of resources—a psychologist, a social worker."

Time and Place

Principals need to make the time, and be available, best placing themselves in the halls before school and in classrooms, during school. As one teacher explained: "If teachers come at the very start of the term, they get a weeklong orientation provided by the district. Part of that, they have *time with the principal* so that we can share our philosophy, our expectations. We have a faculty manual that everybody gets on the first day; give it back at the end of the year."

Principals are becoming more aware of the importance of orienting teachers to their schools rather than to a general or even district-defined concept of school. In discussions with the six principals who had participated in the NJCUE professional development program, one said,

> Presently, the new teachers go to the district orientation. That doesn't help them feel comfortable in our school. I would like to take on that responsibility of working with new teachers. I don't think the district believes that principals want that responsibility. Maybe a compromise would work: the district could do the orientation for human resources (salaries and benefits), but we could have more time to orient teachers to our specific situation—in our place and our time!

Common Planning Time

Not only was there general agreement regarding the need for interaction and support from the principal, but all novices cried out for greater collaboration with fellow teachers. However, several teachers reported that finding the time to work together presented a challenge. As one said, "I find talking to the other math teachers and seeing what they do very helpful, but that's on your own time. It's very difficult because there's no common planning time, so maybe you talk about it over lunch or while you're on supervision or other times like that."

While all schools had in place scheduled times during which groups of teachers met (e.g., grade level meetings, school committee meetings, and professional learning communities), these meetings received mixed reviews from the focus groups. Some were favorable. One said, "In the lower grades, we're all teaching the same thing, so our grade level meetings are very helpful. We share lesson plans, talk about common problems. They're really good." Another remarked, "As a resource teacher, I was able to meet with other fourth-grade teachers and we were able to talk about students some of the time. And that meant a lot to me. Some of those teachers had taught those students the year before and could tell me how they performed last year."

Some were on the fence about the group time: "I think it depends on your group. There are some better groups than others." And some were negative: One said: "Yes, they're mandatory, but not everyone attends. They're mandatory for us, too, but the head of our grade level doesn't really do them. Almost everyone, kind of, shows up, so we'll sit and chitchat." And another:

> However, once you've learned who your students are, it does not take a long time to identify [student] strengths and weaknesses. We need to move past that point. What strategies and techniques can we use now knowing the strengths and weaknesses to improve? Let's talk about it. Let's try it and then let's come back and do a follow-up. And that consistency has not really been there. It seems like every other grade level meeting we're talking about strengths and weaknesses. We never come to any kind of closure about that as a group.

Another explained:

> I don't think the whole committee thing was effective. A lot of us were bamboozled into it. Because in the beginning, they started out saying, "yeah, like guys it's your choice, yea or nay, whatever." But then it went from your choice to mandatory. So people were going there who didn't really want to be there anyway. At first, you had a choice. But then from 8 to 8:30 you have to be somewhere and your vice principals are going to walk around to see if you're there. The problem was there were like 30 of us on one committee. I don't think you can get anything done with that many people. Everyone was giving his or her ideas: "I want to do this." "I want to do that." "Oh no, we can't do that." And then nothing got done.... Somehow the committee meetings were more mandatory than grade level meetings. It used to be every morning we would support each other. Most of us would prefer to have the time to do our own work.

Relationships, Resources, and Reliability

Interestingly, when asked about the support they received from their principals, almost all novices described their principals as supportive if student discipline were handled well and if they had adequate supplies and equipment. Many teachers believed that their schools did not have clear and consistent responses to managing student behavior. One said: "There's not enough support from the administration regarding discipline. The administrators are good people but if you send a kid to them, they just pat them on the head and send them back. It doesn't work." And another: "The administration doesn't enforce the rules. There are no consequences for bad behavior. There's no support for teachers. We have to swipe in. [There's a time clock.] It's more like an adversarial relationship."

The shortage of supplies and equipment was a common concern along with the widespread belief that belt tightening was taking place and things were getting worse: "The school administration is supportive, but the supply situation is not great. And our computers are so old. They have no USB ports. The kids can't really use them."

And another:

> Our new principal is much better interpersonally, but supplies are limited. It's difficult to get supplies. My classroom has eight computers, but only four work. Last year, we had a tech person, but now we have to request one from the district [Jersey City] and wait and wait. I would like to use the computers a lot more.

And a third:

> At the beginning of the year, we had nothing, NOTHING! We got math books at the beginning of January. The district said the order needed to be "justified." It's a little better now, but the supplies are still meager. We have three computers, but two are broken and the printer is broken too.

Several teachers in one of the participating districts mentioned getting some of their most essential school supplies from outside sources. "The supplies in the school are not so good, but from Title I we can get them from the New Jersey Community Food Bank. I get most of my supplies there." And, "Supplies are not readily available in school. I go to the food bank in Hillside. I can go twice a year. I get points to spend and I can get basic supplies and, for example, book bags for incentives."

Many teachers continued to complain that administrators did not offer sufficient support to special education teachers, such as providing them with time for their own meetings. There was fairly widespread sentiment that administrators lacked an understanding of the special education model and could benefit from additional training. "On the one hand, special education kids are not a priority for this administration. But there's pressure to pass the [New Jersey Assessment of Skills and Knowledge]. And they don't recognize that special education kids are not at grade level." And another: "Our principal doesn't understand anything about special ed. His expectations are ridiculous. He needs to take some courses so he could understand what's going on in our classrooms."

And another:

> This is the third administration since I've been in this school. They keep changing because the school performance is bad. They come in with different styles of management, but I haven't seen any improvement. There's no support from the administration. There are some supplies, but not a lot. I have to buy them on my own. I won't stay in this profession. My first two years have been crappy.

Turning to Colleagues Rather Than to Their Principal

Most teachers attributed growth to assistance from colleagues rather than support from their principals. Several special education teachers credited their school's inclusion specialist for helping them improve their classroom management skills. While one teacher mentioned a supervisor as being instrumental in helping her with classroom management issues, the overwhelming majority of focus group participants felt the biggest influence on their growth came from fellow teachers. "I've grown mainly by working with colleagues; watching what they do, fine-tuning it for myself."

"I've always cotaught with another teacher, and so we're able to bounce ideas off each other. That's been the biggest thing helping me grow." "If [another teacher in the school] wasn't in my classroom, I wouldn't have survived. I was just put into that classroom and told don't let it fall apart. She has constantly helped me—text messaging back and forth at night—I'm trying to do my lesson plans and I have this problem."

The general feeling among the teachers was well captured by the teacher who said:

> Where I start in September is never where I finish in June, and that's because of the resources I get from my colleagues. Just to be able to have a wealth of years of experience in the building and teachers sharing ideas and information, that's just invaluable to me. The greatest thing I've been able to glean from as I've grown as a teacher—definitely other teachers.

Being Mentored and Growing, Sometimes

New teachers reported mixed experiences with their assigned mentors. Some found the experiences to be poor and useless:

> My mentor was terrible. He was a retired principal who thought he knew everything, and he wanted everything done his way. He didn't know anything about

math, which is what I was teaching. But it didn't matter; he just told me what to do, and of course it didn't work because he didn't know what he was talking about.

Most negative anecdotes about mentoring experiences involved those teachers who never received a mentor, or who were given a mentor only after many months of teaching. There was little understanding among the teachers about why some people got assigned mentors and some did not. "They gave me a mentor on my contract, but that same mentor in September was out on leave because she was retiring. She wasn't even in the building." And, "I didn't get my NJCUE mentor until half the year was over. That was a real big problem because you had to sink or swim until you learned to adapt by yourself. It's like when the mentor came in and said maybe you should try doing this or that, well, super, but that ship already sailed."

In contrast, others stressed the vitality and importance of their mentor to their lives as new teachers.

> I had the greatest mentor. She held my hand, gave me helpful teaching tips, made sure that I got all the information that I needed. She even did research online for me. She provided so much support. By the end of the year, she was a friend.

Many deemed frequent and convenient meeting times for mentors and mentees as the most critical, and often absent, structure.

> My mentor was very helpful, very informative. What interfered with her being even more effective is time. Time did not afford either of us the opportunity to get together more often to discuss certain issues. If I have a question or have a concern, she makes herself available, but I think she could be more effective if more time was allotted for us to meet. We have no common prep period. I think they should better plan for mentoring partnerships; they should strategically plan so that the mentoring really takes place, because my mentor, while I can go find her, there isn't a specific time when we sit down and really have quality time together so she could be more supportive. They should arrange that we meet on a regular schedule.

DISCUSSION AND CONCLUSIONS

Learning to Teach

New Teacher Learning: Alone in a Crowd

The nonroutine nature of teaching challenges the belief that preservice preparation programs are sufficient to support teacher induction. On Day 1, and throughout their careers, novices are faced with making more than 3,000 nontrivial decisions each day (Danielson, 1996). And, as described by these

New Jersey novices, like all teachers they have enormous authority within their classrooms although their skills are underdeveloped and their tools are limited (Lipsky, 1980).

The practices teachers construct over time depend heavily on the meanings they ascribe to the everyday events in their classrooms (Van den Berg, 2002). Yet as novices, they often find that they have little or no basis for sorting out content or for ascertaining which content is relatively more or less important (Kennedy, 2004).

Despite their accountability to the principal, teachers regularly engage in private, unobserved activity that provides them with enormous curricular, instructional, and assessment autonomy. For some novices, practice makes perfect (Britzman, 1991), as they hold on to the initial strategies that they brought with them to their early days with students. For others, their own primary and secondary school experiences in other people's classrooms, better described by Lortie (1975) as their apprenticeship of observation, trump the more reform-minded practices that they may have learned in their certification programs.

Because teachers spend most of their time with children rather than with other educators, they develop their understanding of effective practice by looking in a one-way mirror. The novices in this study clearly reported a keen interest in working with colleagues; few, however, reported that the structures in their schools supported the opportunities they sought (Deal, Purinton, & Waetjean, 2009).

Espoused Theory versus Theory in Use

The findings identify important differences between the teaching orientations that teachers self-profess, that principals believe they hold, and that an external review of their practices suggests. Argyris and Schön (1996) describe the ways in which teachers' practices often differ from the kinds of practices they espouse; as Kennedy (2004) argued, they may describe their own practices as more consistent with reform ideals than outside observers believe to be the case (see Cohen's [1990] memorable description of Mrs. Oublier).

Further, given the limits of their skills and knowledge, they often struggle with the gap between what they hope to do (their intentions or aspirations) and what they are able to put into place. In the early years, while they are developing the principles of their own practice, they need systematic feedback from peers, from more experienced and expert colleagues, and, *most importantly, from their school leaders*. They are not always ready to select the practices most likely to support student learning. While their intentions and interests often align with reform ideals, their practices may not.

Learning to Teach in a High-Stakes Accountability Environment

Initial enthusiasm for the benefits of collegiality and collaboration has been tempered by skepticism (Hargreaves, 1993; Little, 1990). From a psychological viewpoint, classroom isolation offers teachers a measure of privacy and protection from outside interference (Hargreaves, 1993), including interference that comes in the form of high-stakes testing carrots and sticks.

Consequently, isolation was a self-imposed state and a desirable practice, another strategy for teachers to use at the appropriate time. Importantly, then, as accountability stakes increase, novices may find that their veteran colleagues have less time to devote to newcomers' development. Further, Winkler's (2002) research suggests that novice and veteran teachers hold very distinct views regarding the value and effects of high-stakes testing. His research argues that novices believe that standardized testing programs provide them with multiple benefits, including a consistent curriculum, meaningful opportunities for collaboration, and a license for pedagogical freedom within the framework of the standards.

As new teachers, they report feeling greater self-efficacy and certainty in their roles in standards-bearing schools. In contrast, Winkler (2002) determined that experienced teachers were challenged by the current press for standards and high-stakes standardized assessments, finding the testing regimen both threatening and freedom reducing (see also Meier, 2002). Consequently, at the very moment that novices assert their interest in working with and learning from expert veterans, their more experienced colleagues appear to be out of sight, seeking protection from the external onslaught of high-stakes testing. *Unless principals create the structures and cultures for new collaborative interactions, the novices may not find school-based opportunities for learning.*

THE PRINCIPAL'S ROLE

The findings from these two studies support considerable prior research in relation to the role that novices hope their principals will play during their selection, induction, and long-term development. The most salient findings focus on the school's hiring process and practices; the culture, structures, and resources for teacher learning; and their opportunities for leadership and decision making.

Hiring

When new teachers experience a hiring process that gives them a comprehensive and accurate preview of their jobs, they are more likely to derive job satisfaction (Liu, 2004). In a related study, Levin and Quinn (2003) found that late-summer hiring practices in four urban districts starkly contrasted with those of their surrounding districts.

Teacher-to-Teacher Learning

The principal plays a central role in altering the work relationships of teachers. Little (1982) found that the prevalence of collegiality in a school was closely related to specific behaviors of the principal. Collegiality was enhanced when the principal (1) stated expectations explicitly for cooperation among teachers; (2) modeled collegiality by working with teachers and other principals to improve schools; (3) rewarded collegiality by recognizing teachers and granting release time, materials, or funds to teachers who worked as colleagues; and (4) "protected" collaborating teachers from external distractions and unnecessary demands.

In researching schools as a workplace, Rosenholtz (1989) established the centrality of the principal in working with teachers to shape the school as a collaborative workplace by developing shared goals and learning opportunities for teachers. Most notably, principals engineered norms of collaboration and communicated that teaching was a collective rather than an individual activity.

Building Novices' Capacity through Internal Accountability

Newman, King, and Rigdon (1997) found that schools with strong internal accountability systems—including the means for staff to identify standards for student performance, collect data to measure their progress, and use peer review to drive goal attainment—were more likely to increase their organizational capacity.

They also found that organizational capacity rested on teachers' professional knowledge and skill, effective leadership, availability of technical and financial resources, organizational autonomy to act according to demands of local context, and the effective and collective management of the human, technical, and social resources of a school. Most importantly, in schools in which practice is public, novices are less likely to hide their challenges from others.

Teacher and Student Learning Require an Orderly Climate

Rosenholtz (1989) determined that more than half of teacher one-day absenteeism could be explained by their learning opportunities, their psychic rewards, and the school's management of student behavior. As described by some of our novices who work in schools where order is low and student underachievement is high, teachers' "pride is rubbed raw" (Metz, 1993, p. 105). Yet, on the other hand, when classroom order displaces learning as the definition of teaching success, teachers cannot derive the psychic rewards that sustain them and deepen their commitment to student learning (Lortie, 1975).

Schools that have begun successfully to manage behaviorally challenging students define the issue of student discipline as a shared responsibility. *In contrast to novices who work in schools where they feel that their principals are sending students back to classrooms with a "pat on the head," in schools where faculty and staff assist each other in enforcing the schools' standards for student behavior, individual teachers feel that they are not alone in confronting students' noncompliance and misconduct* (Denscombe, 1985).

Principal Invisibility and Isolation

New teachers in integrated professional cultures describe their principals as visibly engaged in both the daily life of the school and the professional work of the teachers (Kardos, Johnson, Peske, Kauffman, & Liu, 2001). These principals focus on the improvement of teaching and learning, visit classrooms, and provide feedback. They arrange school schedules so that expert teachers are able to teach model lessons or meet with new teachers one-on-one or in small groups.

Although teachers have been described as artisans, as bricoleurs (Levi-Strauss, 1966) who "work alone, learn alone, and who derive the most important professional satisfaction alone" (Huberman, 1990, p. 12), the academic success of children and youth depends upon the wisdom of practice that most novices do not yet possess. They cannot be successful on their own; they need opportunities to engage in practices that are public, supported by their more expert peers and their school leaders.

Like other researchers studying teacher effectiveness (see a large-scale study recently completed by Palardy & Rumberger, 2008), we believe that teachers' attitudes and instructional practices strongly predict student learning. Yet in this study, we discovered that teachers and administrators seem to characterize practice differently. One might argue that the administrators' view is most "accurate" given that teachers may be reporting on what they hope to do rather than on what they do. But at the same time, we know that most administrators themselves only have access to a limited amount of information about teachers' practices.

The different ratings given, while open to multiple interpretations, seem to argue for principals and teachers to spend time together in developing a shared vision of what good teaching is. For this to happen, principals need to spend much more time in novice teachers' classrooms than they currently allocate.

Like teachers, school-based administrators have been socialized to being on their own, working hard at what they do while expecting and receiving little support from others (Cuban, 1990). These norms, however, are not conducive to building individual skills or group learning.

TEACHER WORK REDESIGN, TEACHER LEADERSHIP, AND THE LIMITS OF TEACHER-TO-TEACHER COLLABORATION

For more than twenty years, reformers have directed considerable effort toward improving schools by expanding teachers' work roles (e.g., Holmes Group, 1986). They reminded us that teachers' work was often lonely, unsupported, and uncertain. By expanding teachers' roles, increasing their work complexity, and creating collegial work environments, reformers sought to re-create schools by redesigning teachers' tasks.

However, like their experienced peers elsewhere, the veteran teachers across New Jersey's urban schools prize their individuality (Hargreaves, 1993). While we did not directly examine experienced teachers' values, beliefs, and practices in these studies, they are probably like their peers elsewhere who describe their overarching commitments to self and students, rather than to the workplace or to the development of others (Huberman, 1993; Lortie, 1975; Prawat, 1991).

If principals seek to engage their expert teacher colleagues in the development of novices, they will need to understand the ways in which teacher leaders have described their newly expanded roles. While many see this expansion as providing them with significant opportunities for personal and professional growth, others reveal the "dark side" of their new roles, including the assumption of more work, increased responsibilities, and more conflicts (e.g., Smylie & Denny, 1993). While some teachers have reported examples of greater voice (shared decision making), and increased compensation (stipends for their new out-of-the-classroom jobs), teacher work redesign has not changed the norms of "real school" (see Metz description, 1990). Ironically, the addition of out-of-classroom responsibilities for novice colleagues does not necessarily provide more senior teachers with the opportunities to deepen and improve their own practices.

The teachers and principals who provided information for this evaluation work in three of New Jersey's largest urban school districts. As reported herein, structures for collaboration vary by school and even by grade level.

Even among those teachers who explained having access to peers through scheduled common planning times, teachers and school leaders reflected that structures were necessary but insufficient to guarantee teacher development.

In ways that echo the findings of those who have examined the promise of peer-to-peer learning among youngsters (e.g., Rohrbeck, Ginsburg-Block, Fantuzzo, & Miller, 2003; Stevens & Slavin, 1995), novice teachers need to learn how to work effectively with peers and their more veteran colleagues. Without access to that learning, and modeling by the veteran teacher leaders, teachers will continue to value individual tasks and prefer work that keeps them isolated from colleagues, thereby promoting privatism and professional autonomy.

The reflections by novices in this study suggest that their schools are like other schools with highly experienced teachers; thus, it will take a particular set of skills, resources, and professional development for teacher and administrator leaders to develop collaborative cultures among professionals who have already developed strong norms of independence and autonomy.

Developing Systems to Support Novice Learning: Building In-School Mentoring Systems

While many researchers cite the importance of mentors' attitudes and interpersonal skills (see Feiman-Nemser & Parker, 1993; Gibb & Welch, 1998), less attention has been provided to identifying the knowledge, skills, and dispositions that mentors need to demonstrate in their own classrooms in order to be selected for and supported in their mentoring roles. Overwhelming evidence supports the notion that effective mentors are trained for their job and that the training and support must be an ongoing process.

Experienced Teachers' Commitment

Recent research has linked teacher commitment to the professional development phase of their work lives. The research suggests different levels of teacher commitment in their early, middle, and later careers, with the commitment of those in their later careers more at risk (e.g., Day, Sammons, & Gu, 2008, p. 337). This finding, once again, supports previous research that identifies distinct phases in teachers' professional lives (Huberman, 1990, 1993), and the proposition that the retention of experienced teachers may depend upon the creation of differentiated roles for teachers in this period of their work.

Most importantly, the Day et al. study (2008) argues that irrespective of school context features, it is more likely that students will attain results at or above the expected levels when their teachers feel effective and committed.

School cultures in which the prevailing orientation is commitment rather than control require specific opportunities for learning, growth, voice, and choice for adults and the students in their classes.

GOING FORWARD

The development and retention of quality novice teachers are heralded as both the problem and the solution to the underachievement of America's children and youth. Yet solutions are elusive, as the revolving novice teacher door simultaneously drains urban district coffers[1] and limits the potential for student learning. It will take a unique form of collaboration and cross-organizational commitment to change teaching from a flat career governed by norms that privilege peer equality over differentiated roles for differently able and interested professionals.

Reinventing teaching from a semiprofession (Etzioni, 1969) in which entrants sink or swim to a full profession in which each novice is provided with systematic and ongoing feedback and support will take more than legislated "mentoring." This reinvention will challenge the sacred beliefs and taken-for-granted behaviors of teachers and school leaders. Doing nothing, however, will guarantee the loss of thousands of teachers and the failure of millions of students.

The implications for school leaders are important too, including their becoming more readily available, concerned, and skilled as teacher mentors and masters of teaching, and being more keenly aware of the needs of new teachers (see Varrati, Lavine, & Turner, 2009 for the description of a new conceptual model for principal involvement in teacher education). This study showed how important the first few months are to new teachers and how orientations need to be local and school centered, since each school has its own culture and mentoring support systems. Principals should be available, consistently and often, to see that teachers are developing strong new relationships and that they have the necessary resources to do their jobs.

Universities and other training groups need to put the teacher, classroom, and students back at the center of leader preparation: they should require principals-in-training to visit classrooms, bring teachers into the prep programs, and reaffirm that teachers often feel alone, and new teachers especially feel really isolated. It's the principal's first job, as a leader, to hook up with teachers and get them organized in "learning communities" with mentor teachers and in working groups with other new teachers.

It's a team effort from start to finish: universities teaching new administrators to see communities of new and old teachers and instructing how to build and sustain them, and administrator internships involving trainees in weaving the web of support in their schools. New teachers need to work closely with other teachers, and administrators, from the beginning in their schools. And principals new on the job should find time and space to build mentoring communities and visit them in action. We know this is happening when a principal can walk into a new teacher's classroom and no one notices—since it's become a regular occurrence.

One new principal put it this way: "I want to create a climate where teachers open the doors and allow others to come in, without anxiety, like it's a gotcha . . . To me, the more specific you get, the greater the value." It's about caring for new teachers, creating a community and sharing environment, and helping teachers to help themselves and one another. This view of the school, and its leaders, is the heart of making schools better places to work and grow.

NOTE

1. The U.S. Department of Labor estimates the cost per teacher at $12,546.

REFERENCES

Allenwood Company (2008). *A tale of two studies*. Program Evaluation completed for the New Jersey Consortium of Urban Education. Montclair, New Jersey.

Argyris, C., & D. A. Schön (1996). *Organizational learning II*. New York: Addison Wesley.

Bennett, N., & Carré, C. (1993). *Learning to teach*. London: Routledge.

Black, J. K., & Puckett, M. (1996). *The young child: Development from pre-birth through age eight* (2nd ed.). Englewood Cliffs, NJ: Prentice Hall.

Britton, E., Paine, L., Raizen, S., & Pimm, D. (2003). *Comprehensive teacher induction: Systems for early career learning*. Norwell, MA: Kluwer Academic Publishers and WestEd.

Britzman, D. (1991). *Practice makes practice*. New York: Teachers College Press.

Brown, K. M., & Wynn, S. R. (2007). Teacher retention issues: How some principals are supporting and keeping new teachers. *Journal of School Leadership, 17*, 664–698.

Cohen, D. K. (1990). A revolution in one classroom: The case of Mrs. Oublier. *Educational Evaluation and Policy Analysis, 12*(3), 311–329.

Colbert, J. A., & Wolff, D. E. (1992). Surviving in urban schools: A collaborative model for a beginning teacher support system. *Journal of Teacher Education, 44*(3), 193–200.

Cuban, L. (1990). Reforming again, again, and again. *Educational Researcher, 19*(1), 3–13.

Cummins, J. (1999). Alternative paradigms in bilingual education research: Does theory have a place? *Educational Researcher, 28*(7), 26–41.

Cummins, J. (2009). A response to "Developing Literacy in Second-Language Learners." *Educational Researcher, (38)*5, 385.

Danielson, C. (1996). *Enhancing professional practice: A framework for teaching.* Alexandria, VA: Association for Supervision & Curriculum Development.

Day, D., Sammons, P., & Gu, Q. (2008). Combining quantitative and qualitative methodologies in research on teachers' lives, work, and effectiveness: From integration to synergy. *Educational Researcher, 37*(6), 330–342.

Deal, T. E., Purinton, T., & Waetjean, D. C. (2009). *Making sense of social networks in schools.* Thousand Oaks, CA: Sage.

Denscombe, M. (1985). *Classroom control: A sociological perspective.* London: Allen & Unwin.

Etzioni, A. (Ed.) (1969). *The semi-professions and their organization: Teachers, nurses, social workers.* New York: Free Press.

Feiman-Nemser, S., & Parker, M. B. (1993). Mentoring in context: A comparison of two U.S. programs for beginning teachers. *International Journal of Educational Research, 19,* 699–718.

Fideler, E., & Haselkorn, D. (1999*). Learning the ropes: Urban teacher induction programs and practices in the United States.* Belmont, MA: Recruiting New Teachers.

Gallacher, K. K. (1997). Supervision, mentoring, and coaching: Methods for supporting personnel development. In P. J. Winton, J. A. McCollum, and C. Catlett (Eds.), *Reforming personnel preparation in early intervention: Issues, models, and practical strategies* (pp. 191–214). Baltimore: Brookes.

Gibb, G., & Welch, M. (1998). The Utah mentor teacher academy: Evaluation of a statewide mentor program. *Teacher Education and Special Education, 21*(1), 22-33.

Hargreaves, A. (1993). Individualism and individuality: Reinterpreting the teacher culture. In J. W. Little and M. W. McLaughlin, (Eds.), *Teachers' work: Individuals, colleagues and contexts* (pp. 51–76). New York: Teachers College Press.

Henry, J. S., Stockdate, M. S., Hall, M., & Deniston, W. (1994). A formal mentoring program for junior female faculty: Description and evaluation. *Journal of NAWE, 56*(2), 37–45.

Holmes Group, The. (April 1986). *Tomorrow's teachers: A report of the Holmes Group.* East Lansing, MI: Holmes Group Incorporated.

Houston, W. R., McDavid, T., & Marshall, F. (1990). A study of the induction of 300 first-year teachers and their mentors, 1989–1990. Texas Education Agency, Houston Independent School District & University of Houston. (ERIC Document Reproduction Services No. 338558.)

Huberman, M. (1990). *The social context of instruction in schools.* Boston: American Educational Research Association Annual Meeting.

Huberman, M. (1993). The model of the independent artisan in teachers' professional relations. In J. W. Little and M. W. McLaughlin, (Eds*.), Teachers' work: Individuals, colleagues and contexts,* (pp. 11–50). New York: Teachers College Press.

Huling-Austin, L. (1990). Teacher induction programs and internships. In W. R. Houston (Ed.) *Handbook of research on teacher education*. Reston, VA: Association of Teacher Educators.

Huling-Austin, L. (1992). Research on learning to teach: Implications for teacher induction and mentoring programs. *Journal of Teacher Education, 43*(3), 173-180.

Kardos, S. M. (2004). *Supporting and sustaining new teachers in schools: The importance of professional culture and mentoring*. Cambridge, MA: Harvard University.

Kardos, S. M., Johnson, S. M., Peske, H. G., Kauffman, D., & Liu, E. (2001). Counting on colleagues: New teachers encounter the professional cultures of their schools. *Educational Administration Quarterly, 37*(2), 250–290.

Kennedy, M. M. (2004, April 7). Reform ideals and teachers' practical intentions. *Education Policy Analysis Archives, 12*(13). Retrieved from http://epaa.asu.edu/epaa/v12n13

Levi-Strauss, C. (1966). *The savage mind*. London: Weidenfeld and Nicholson.

Levin, J., & Quinn, M. (2003). *Missed opportunities: How we keep high-quality teachers out of urban schools*. New York: The New Teacher Project.

Lipsky, M. (1980). *Street-level bureaucracy: Dilemmas of the individual in public services*. New York: Russell Sage Foundation.

Little, J. (1982). Norms of collegiality and experimentation: Workplace conditions of school success. *American Educational Research Journal, 19*(3), 325–340.

Little, J. W. (1990). The persistence of privacy: Autonomy and initiative in teachers' professional relations. *Teachers College Record, 91*(4), 509–536.

Liu, E. (2004). *New teachers' experiences of hiring in four states*. Cambridge, MA: Harvard University.

Lortie, D. (1975). *Schoolteacher: A sociological study*. Chicago: University of Chicago Press.

McCormick, K. M., & Brennan, S. (2001). Mentoring the new professional in interdisciplinary early childhood education: The Kentucky teacher internship program. *Topics in Early Childhood Special Education, 21*(3), 131–149.

Meier, D. (2002). Standardization versus standards. *Phi Delta Kappan, 84*(3), 190–198.

Metz, M. (1990). Real school: A universal drama amid disparate experience. In D. E. Mitchell & M. E., Goertz (Eds.), (pp. 75–91). London: The Falmer Press.

Metz, M. H. (1993). Teachers' ultimate dependence on their students. In J. W. Little and M. W. McLaughlin (Eds.), *Teachers' work: Individuals, colleagues and contexts,* (pp. 104–136). New York: Teachers College Press.

Newman, F. M., King, M. B., & Rigdon, M. (1997). Accountability and school performance: Implications from restructuring schools. *Harvard Educational Review, 67*(1), 41–57.

Odell, S. J., & Ferraro, D. P. (1992). Teacher mentoring and teacher retention. *Journal of Teacher Education, 43*(3), 200–204.

Palardy, G. J., & Rumberger, R. W. (2008). Teacher effectiveness in first grade: The importance of background qualifications, attitudes, and instructional practices for student learning. *Educational Evaluation and Policy Analysis, 30*(2): 111–140.

Prawat, R. S. (1991). Conversations with self and settings: A framework for thinking about teacher empowerment. *American Educational Research Journal, 28*(4), 737-757.

Ragins, B. R., Cotton, J. L., & Miller, J. S. (2000). Marginal mentoring: The effects of type of mentor, quality of relationship, and program design on work and career attitudes. *Academy of Management Journal, 43*(6), 1177–1194.

Rohrbeck, C. A., Ginsburg-Block, M. D., Fantuzzo, J. W., & Miller, T. R. (2003). Peer-assisted learning interventions with elementary school students: A meta-analytic review. *Journal of Educational Psychology, 95*(2), 240–257.

Rosenholtz, S. J. (1989). *Teachers' workplace.* New York: Longman, Inc.

Schlager, M., Fusco, J., Koch, M., Crawford, V., & Phillips, M. (2003, July). Designing equity and diversity into online strategies to support new teachers. Paper presented at the National Educational Computing Conference (NECC), Seattle, WA.

Smylie, M. A., & Denny, J. W. (1993). Teacher leadership: Tensions and ambiguities in organizational perspective. *Educational Administration Quarterly, 26*(3), 235–239.

Stevens, R. J., & Slavin, R. E. (1995). The cooperative elementary school: Effects on students' achievement, attitudes, and social relations. *American Educational Research Journal, 32*(2), 321–351.

Van den Berg, B. (2002). Teachers' meanings regarding educational practice. *Review of Educational Research, 72*(4), 577–625.

Varrati, A. M., Lavine, M. E., & Turner, S. L. (2009). A new conceptual model for principal involvement and professional collaboration in teacher education. *Teachers College Record, 111*(2), 480–510.

Winkler, A. (2002). Division in the ranks: Standardized testing draws lines between new and veteran teachers. *Phi Delta Kappan, 84*(3), 219–225.

Wong, H. K. (2004). Induction programs that keep new teachers teaching and improving. *NASSP Bulletin, 87*(638), 5–27.

Chapter Four

Midcareer Teachers and Principals

William H. Marinell

To be successful in their roles, tomorrow's educational leaders will need to enter schools with an extensive set of skills and knowledge. Successful educational leadership in the years and decades ahead will require both creativity and managerial prowess, the ability to analyze data and forge partnerships with local organizations, and the capability to draw promising new teachers to schools, support their development, and capitalize on their skills. For leaders in urban schools, where teaching vacancies are hard to fill and rates of teacher mobility and attrition are often high, accomplishing these latter goals related to recruitment and retention will be all the more challenging.

To make matters more complicated—though potentially more rewarding for schools—the composition of the teacher workforce is changing. Tomorrow's leaders will have to recruit and support teachers who have pursued different preparation programs, possess a range of skills and experiences, and come from a variety of professional and academic backgrounds.

In recent years, policy makers and researchers have identified one particular subgroup of teachers, midcareer entrants—teachers who enter the profession after having worked in fields other than teaching—as a population of teachers who may help tomorrow's leaders address a number of these challenges. Policy makers have heralded midcareer entrants' potential to help improve teacher quality—and thus raise student achievement—by bringing valuable content knowledge and organizational insight to schools (American Competitiveness Initiative, 2006; National Academies Press, 2000, 2005; Johnson, Birkeland, Donaldson, Kardos, Kauffman, Liu, & Peske, 2004). Researchers have asserted that midcareer entrants might help fill hard-to-staff vacancies in urban schools and in subjects like secondary math and science (Natriello & Zumwalt, 1993; American Competitiveness Initiative, 2006), as well as reduce the racial and gender imbalances that exist between teachers and students in U.S. public schools by bringing more males and minorities into teaching (Feistritzer, 2005; Ruenzel, 2002; Shen, 1997, 1998).

While there is substantial enthusiasm about midcareer entrants' potential, there is little research for administrators to draw on to help them understand how midcareer entrants may be altering the characteristics of the teacher workforce and, more practically, how midcareer entrants might change the way schools operate in the future. Even the most basic questions administrators might have about midcareer entrants remain unanswered, questions such as: How many midcareer entrants are entering teaching? What personal characteristics, professional skills, and experiences are they bringing with them to their schools?

A number of these questions are addressed in this chapter. To establish the relevant background and context related to midcareer entrants, this chapter briefly summarizes the literature and presents an overview of a quantitative investigation (publication forthcoming) of a large, national data set.

Subsequently, the chapter presents and discusses findings from an exploratory study of the skills and knowledge that ten math and science midcareer entrants brought to their schools. The objective of the chapter is to help tomorrow's building- and district-level leaders consider how the changing composition of the teacher workforce may require that they develop new, differentiated strategies for recruiting talented teachers, supporting their development in schools, and capitalizing on their skills.

BACKGROUND AND CONTEXT

Midcareer entrants' presence in the public school teacher workforce is a relatively recent phenomenon, first observed in the late 1980s when graduate school admissions officers discovered that applicants to teacher preparation programs were becoming increasingly older and more experienced (Novak & Knowles, 1992; Crow, Levine, & Nager, 1990; Tift, 1989). In the three decades prior, most new teachers entered the profession immediately after graduating from college and remained in teaching for the duration of their career (Spencer, 2001; Grant & Murray, 1999; Murnane, Singer, Willett, Kemple, & Olsen, 1991; Rury, 1989).

Subsequent evidence supported admissions officers' anecdotal observations. Feistritzer (1999) reported that between the late 1980s and late 1990s, the percentage of teacher preparation programs that enrolled postbaccalaureate applicants jumped from 3% to over 25%. Broughman and Rollefson (2000) reported that the percentage of the public school teaching force that were newly hired "delayed entrants"[1] increased from 9.3% in 1987–1988 to 15.3% in 1990–1991 and to 16.6% in 1993–1994. More recently, Johnson et al. (2004) found that in randomly drawn samples of first- and second-year public school teachers in seven U.S. states, between 28% and 47% were midcareer entrants.

While few studies are explicit about the criteria that were used to identify the midcareer teachers of interest, nearly all share the common understanding that midcareer entrants are distinct from first-career entrants, the latter of whom usually obtain their certification credentials directly after graduating from college and then immediately become teachers. In addition, some studies (e.g., Broughman & Rollefson, 2000; Johnson et al., 2004; Crow et al., 1990) imply that midcareer entrants are distinct from "reentrants"—those who take a break in their teaching service before reentering teaching—and from those who enter teaching later in life but still as a first career, which is common among women who raise children before becoming teachers. Lastly, some studies (e.g., Johnson et al., 2004) either state or suggest that to be considered a midcareer entrant, one must have worked in his or her prior career for a substantial period of time—at the very least, five years.

Historically, policy makers have been interested in both the role that midcareer entrants can play in staffing public schools and in their potential for improving the quality of teaching and learning in the schools where they teach. Much of this interest has been driven by the mathematics and science community, which has suggested that midcareer entrants might help address both the persistent shortages of qualified teachers in these subject areas and the poor student performance that have plagued public school mathematics and science education in the post-Sputnik era (American Competitiveness Initiative, 2006; National Academies Press, 2000, 2005; NCMST, 2000; Natriello & Zumwalt, 1992).

To date, policy makers' assertions about midcareer entrants' potential to invigorate teaching have been based largely on conjecture and loosely related research on teachers' academic backgrounds. Some evidence shows that midcareer entrants may help improve student performance by attracting individuals from underrepresented subgroups into the public school teacher workforce (Feistritzer, 2005; Chin, Young, & Floyd, 2004; Ruenzel, 2002; Shen, 1998; summarized in Johnson, Birkeland, & Peske, 2005).

Attracting more males and minorities into teaching may have important consequences for student performance, as research suggests that the substantial gender and racial imbalances that exist between teachers and students today have detrimental effects on a variety of student outcomes, such as students' performance on tests and their sense of self-worth (e.g., Wiggan, 2007; Dee, 2004, 2005, 2006; Steele, 1997). Dee (2006) found that students performed better on assessments and were more engaged with their academic material when they were taught by a teacher of the same gender. Analyzing different data, Dee (2004) found a similar relationship between student performance and teachers' race.

A recent analysis of five administrations of the national, cross-sectional Schools and Staffing Surveys (SASS) (1987–88, 1990–1991, 1993–1994, 1999–2000, and 2003–2004) indicates that the percentage of midcareer entrants among first-year teachers nearly doubled—from 20% to 39%—between 1987 and 1988 and 2003 and 2004. Further, midcareer entrants were more likely than first-career entrants to be male and from minority, non-white racial/ethnic backgrounds. Interestingly, however, despite these characteristics, midcareer entrants' increasing presence in the new teacher workforce has not ameliorated the gender imbalance and has played only a partial role in reducing the racial imbalance among first-year teachers.

The findings from this quantitative analysis underscore the importance of learning more about the skills and knowledge that midcareer entrants bring to their schools. Given the sheer number of midcareer entrants in the new teacher workforce, building and district leaders must take pause and consider whether this critical mass of incoming midcareer entrants possess different expectations about how their schools will be run and have different professional development needs and career expectations. Learning more about the skills and knowledge of one particular subgroup of midcareer entrants—those from math and science backgrounds—seems all the more urgent given the persistently low student performance in these areas and the difficulty administrators have in filling math and science vacancies in their schools (e.g., Strizek, Pittsonberger, Riordan, Lyter, & Orlofsky, 2006).

In an effort to learn more about the capabilities and experiences of math and science midcareer entrants, interviews with 10 such teachers who were working in four high schools in the greater Boston area were conducted, seeking to understand whether math and science midcareer entrants' former work had equipped them with the practical understanding of their subjects that policy makers have anticipated. Further, inquiries were made about whether participants brought additional skills from their former work that had eased their transition into teaching. Lastly, the study asked participants to describe the nature of their interactions with colleagues in an effort to determine whether participants had opportunities to share their knowledge and skills.

METHODOLOGY

This exploratory study was conducted with a purposive sample of 10 math and science midcareer entrants who were teaching in the greater Boston area, who were teaching a variety of math- and science-related courses, and who came from a range of math- and science-related industries. Further, participants were teaching in both urban and suburban communities and in schools with different organizational structures (i.e., those organized into traditional subject departments as well as those organized into "small schools" or "academies"). To gather a range of perspectives, efforts were made to maximize the diversity of my sample in terms of age, gender, and race; however, I was unsuccessful in locating non-white participants.

The interviews were conducted of participants at a time when the contrasts between their prior and current careers were clear. Thus, participants were new to teaching but had been teaching long enough to have formed impressions of their new career and work site. On average, participants had been teaching for 5 years and had worked in their previous career for 16 years. Table 4.1 presents summary information about the study participants.

Each midcareer entrant participated in one hour-long, semistructured interview conducted in March or April 2007, asking why they had left their former professions, whether they had worked collaboratively with their colleagues in either career, and whether any skills and knowledge from their former careers had proven useful in teaching. All interviews were conducted in person, audiotaped, and transcribed verbatim.

Thematic summaries were drafted shortly after conducting each interview, followed by analytic memos that identified emergent themes. Transcripts were then revised and expanded these themes based on my coded analyses of the transcripts. From the coded data the analytic memos were refined, and several prominent themes were selected as the foci of this chapter.

This study has several limitations. First, because of the small sample, the findings cannot be generalized to a larger population of math and science midcareer entrants. Second, because interpretations are based solely on participants' self-reports, no additional sources of data were available with which to triangulate participants' claims. Third, because the selected participants had remained in teaching for an average of five years, the study examined a sample with a positive orientation to teaching.

Lastly, outside of Silicon Valley, Boston is considered one of the centers of technological development and scientific research. Given the competitiveness of the Boston market, it is likely that participants' former work sites were

Table 4.1 Participants' Demographic, Subject, and Career-Related Information (Participants Are Grouped by School)

Name	Age	Gender	Subject	Years Teaching	Years in Prior Career	District	School Organization	Prior Career Field
Joe	56	M	Math	3	30	Urban	Departments	Telecommunications
Kate	29	F	Math	3	2	Urban	Departments	Finance
Tim	47	M	Math	4	9	Urban	Small schools	Statistical analysis / consulting
Jerry	52	M	Math	4	28	Urban	Small schools	High-tech
Carter	51	M	Math/ science	5	19	Urban	Small schools	Software programming / management
Marcia	48	F	Math	10	14*	Suburban	Departments	Chemical engineering / technical sales support
Roy	60	M	Math/ science	6	18	Suburban	Departments	Software programming / management
Shelly	51	F	Science	8	14	Suburban	Departments/ houses	Scientific laboratory research
Peg	57	F	Science	4	20	Suburban	Departments/ houses	Electrical engineering
Kerry	30	F	Math	5	2	Suburban	Departments/ houses	Management consulting

* Marcia spent 3 years working as a chemical engineer before her 14-year career in various technical sales support roles.

among the more innovative and demanding in the country. Readers should take these unique aspects of my sample and location into consideration when interpreting these findings.

FINDINGS

The Participants and Their Former Careers

The 10 participants in this study came from a range of math- and science-related industries and held a variety of roles throughout their prior careers. Before becoming teachers, Roy and Carter had worked in computing as programmers, team leaders, and midlevel managers. Both Peg and Jerry had been design and applications engineers in the high-tech industry; in addition, Peg had worked as an electrical engineer and Jerry as a software engineer. Peg and Jerry had also been entry-level "contributors" as well as managers.

Joe and Marcia had spent the majority of their careers working in telecommunications, Joe as a civil engineer and Marcia in technical sales and support. In their prior careers, Shelly had been a researcher at a university-affiliated molecular biology lab, Kate had worked in financial budgeting and forecasting at a large consumer electronics company, and Tim and Kerry had both worked as consultants—Tim at an antitrust and litigation consulting firm and Kerry at a management consulting firm. Most participants whose initial career had spanned more than 5 years had worked for a number of different companies, some notable exceptions being Joe, who worked for the same telecommunications company for 30 years; Shelly, who conducted research at the same laboratory for 14 years; and Tim, who worked as a statistical analyst for the same consulting firm for 9 years.

The characteristics of participants' former work sites varied, though most had spent a portion of their careers working for large national or multinational companies that employed hundreds or thousands—in some cases, tens of thousands—of workers. About half of the participants had worked in companies that differed in terms of size and history. For example, Roy and Carter had worked at small "start-ups" as well as long-established industry giants. Shelly was the only participant who had spent the entirety of her previous career in a relatively small organization; her lab employed about 20 workers, including postdoctoral fellows and technicians.

About half of the sample—including Joe, Kate, Tim, Peg, and to a lesser extent, Marcia—had liked their former work and work sites and had been generally satisfied in their prior careers. Many of the participants within this half of the sample reported finding their work both intellectually challenging and enjoyable. For most of these participants, the decision to change careers was motivated by an interest in either (1) wanting to try a different line of work, (2) finding a job that afforded them more time with their families, or 3) performing work that was more likely to "make a difference" or result in some tangible improvement in the lives of the people with whom they interacted.

The other half of the sample—including Kerry, Shelly, Carter, Jerry, and Roy—had liked some aspects of their former work and work sites but had grown weary, in some cases disgruntled, with others. Many of these participants cited the following qualms with their former work, work sites, or industry: (1) their work, though often challenging and exciting, had been exhaustingly stressful; (2) the cultures of their work sites had been intensely competitive or oppressively hierarchical; or (3) their industry had changed in a way that lessened their interest in their work. While many of these participants had also been seeking more meaningful work and more time with their families, their decision to leave their former career was strongly influenced by their dissatisfaction with their work, work site, or industry.

A number of additional factors influenced participants' decision to leave their former careers and enter teaching. Joe and Kerry discovered that they liked teaching while participating in programs that brought workers from their former employers into classrooms to teach mini-lessons. Peg, Marcia, and Kate discovered their aptitude for teaching while instructing coworkers or clients, or working with student peers during their academic training. Several participants had siblings or friends who were teachers and who spoke enthusiastically of the profession. Others, like Carter, had considered teaching at the outset of their careers but had not entered the field due to long-term financial concerns or immediate financial constraints (e.g., student loans).

Tim's decision to teach had been influenced by the role one important high school teacher had played in cultivating his interest in math; other participants—like Marcia, who had graduated first in a high school class of about 400—had been told by former teachers that their talents would be "wasted" in teaching. Two participants had been laid off during their prior career, an experience that had prompted one to worry about decreasing job security and increasing age discrimination in his industry.

WHAT SKILLS AND KNOWLEDGE DID PARTICIPANTS BRING TO TEACHING?

One of the most common arguments for recruiting math and science midcareer entrants to teaching posits that their professional experience will equip them with a practical understanding of their subject discipline that is superior to the limited book knowledge possessed by their first-career counterparts.

More than one-half of the participants reported bringing practical, subject-related knowledge and skills from their former careers that informed their work as teachers.

Many also indicated that their undergraduate and graduate studies were critical in preparing them with the subject-related knowledge needed to teach. Further, participants reported that they brought additional skills from their former careers—namely technological skills, communication and presentation skills, and grant-writing capabilities—which were also useful to their work as teachers.

Nearly all participants reported bringing extensive subject-related knowledge and skills to teaching. The depth of these capabilities seemed related to two factors: the extent to which participants' former jobs involved working with the subjects they were now teaching, and the undergraduate and graduate degrees participants had obtained in their subject areas. One-half of the sample reported having worked extensively with their subject in their former career. For these participants, strong subject-related knowledge and skills were required to perform organizational tasks. For example, Tim's primary responsibility as a consultant was fitting complex statistical models. Peg's first career as an electrical engineer involved an intimate knowledge of physics and chemistry.

Similarly, Shelly relied on much of the same scientific knowledge—and performed many of the same techniques—in her former work as a molecular biology researcher and in her current work as a science teacher. Several participants had former careers that involved less subject-related work. Several other participants reported that their work required little or no subject-related knowledge or skills at all. For instance, Kerry's work as a management consultant involved "no math."

Despite this variation, all but one of the participants reported feeling well prepared to teach their subjects at the outset of their new careers. Participants indicated that their confidence was strongly influenced by their academic training in their field. All participants had received either an undergraduate and/or graduate degree in a field related to the subjects they were teaching. For example, Roy—now a math teacher—held a bachelor's degree in mathematics and a Ph.D. in computer science. Carter, also a math teacher, had both undergraduate and graduate degrees in physics. Similarly, Shelly held undergraduate and graduate degrees in biology. Kate, a math teacher, had been a finance major in her undergraduate business administration program prior to entering her first career in finance.

Several participants whose former careers had *not* involved working extensively with their subject reported developing analytical skills that were relevant to their work as teachers. For example, Joe, who had performed mainly lightweight "business oriented" math as a telecommunications engineer, reported developing analytical skills from having to perform "reasonability checks" on data that were given to him by his organization's statisticians. Joe learned how to break complex problems into "discrete steps" and to develop processes that allowed him to catch "problems and inconsistencies" in his team's work.

By introducing students to these analytical approaches, Joe thought he could teach students how to "solve any problem." Similarly, Roy discovered that his work as a software programmer involved many of the same analytical processes as the sophisticated math he'd studied in his degree programs. Roy explained, "[As a programmer], I didn't ever implement anything that had to do with a vessel function or a linear algebra theorem, but I was thinking mathematically all the time." He elaborated:

> Everything I did was logic, everything I did was case analysis. Can I prove that this is what happens here? In my head, I'm thinking about the same thing you're doing when you're doing a trig[onometry] identity. I'm taking some program and thinking, "this seems to be a lot of code to do what I need to do. How can I achieve the same goal more efficiently and with less code?" And that's the same thing you do when you're reducing a complex expression to a simpler expression.

Roy found that the analytic skills he developed as a programmer were as valuable to share with his students as the mathematical knowledge he'd gained from his academic training.

Participants described numerous benefits associated with the subject-related knowledge and skills that they brought to teaching. For one, participants' subject-related strengths meant that preparing to teach involved reviewing material rather than learning it for the first time. Moreover, participants' reported having an extensive knowledge base on which to draw when responding to students. Shelly explained:

> I know what I'm talking about when I come into the classroom. . . . I really know how molecular biology is done, how cloning is done, how proteins are analyzed. . . . So there's a real grasp of the material that is second nature up to a point where I just don't have to think about it. And if kids throw me a question, I'm comfortable enough that I can come at it from a million different directions until I'm able to explain things in a way they'll understand. And I'm not sure that I would have that, particularly about something as abstract as molecular biology, if I hadn't been immersed in it for so long.

Nearly all participants reported that their familiarity with their subjects allowed them to generate practical classroom exercises. For example, Jerry introduced students to the coordinates system by describing how it was used in the flight simulators manufactured by one of his previous high-tech employers. Peg introduced concepts to students by first thinking of an illustrative example from her work as an electrical engineer. She described her process:

> I say, "Well, when we were designing power supplies for the first cell phones . . ." or, "Did you ever think about what's going on inside your [cell phone] display?" or, "What do you think about airbags? Now when we were designing the circuitry for airbags . . ."

Carter relied on the mathematical knowledge he had developed as a software programmer and manager, and as an undergraduate and graduate physics major, to generate exercises that he believed were superior to those available in the texts at his large, urban high school.

In addition to garnering, in Peg's words, "credibility and cachet" with students, participants' real-world examples introduced students to the tasks and standards of various math- and science-related careers. Jerry reported that the students in his large, urban high school had "no idea what high-tech [was] about." Thus, developing exercises based on his experience gave students a better sense of the kinds of problems that engineers in this field encountered. Similarly, by explaining to students how a "particular [math] skill played a role in computing," Roy was able to reply to students when they asked, "When are we going to need this in our real lives?"

Roy would respond, "Well, I certainly would not have hired someone to work for me who couldn't prove a geometric identity" and then illustrate how geometry and programming were interrelated. Shelly felt that her experience working in the lab allowed her to teach students professional standards regarding reporting lab results—knowledge that would serve them well if they chose to pursue future scientific work or study.

In addition to their subject-related knowledge and skills, participants also brought a familiarity with technology, grant-writing abilities, and communication and presentation skills that further supported their work as teachers and brought valuable resources to their schools. While participants' subject-related knowledge and skills appeared to benefit their own teaching, these additional capabilities seemed to have benefits that extended beyond the classroom.

Nearly all participants reported bringing a familiarity with technology from their former careers. Their reliance on technology in their prior work made it easy for them to use hardware and software to both organize and execute their work as teachers. For example, as a telecommunications engineer, Joe's "whole career was involved with [technology]."

He used spreadsheet applications to keep track of the logistics of numerous state and national projects. This experience enabled him to "jump right on" and begin using educational technology immediately. Before long, Joe discovered how he could use software programs to link student data (e.g., grades, days absent, etc.) to progress reports. Joe created records that allowed him to inform a student, parent, administrator, or colleague of a student's progress. "It's all here," he said, scrolling through spreadsheets on his computer, " . . . all my grades, days absent, 2005–2006 materials, progress reports, new tests. . . . If I want to look at a summary and see how the kids are doing overall, I can look at this stuff. . . . If a student asks me, 'What do I need to get a B?' I can just plug a number in."

If a parent ever challenged Joe's assertions about her child's performance, Joe could instantaneously present records of the student's work, electronic copies of progress reports that were emailed to the parent, and threads of email correspondence that had occurred between Joe and the parent. He found that the content and organization of his records quickly quelled any disputes.

Beyond aiding in the organization of his work, Joe also found that technology enhanced his instruction and helped hold the interest of his students. He used programs like Geometry Sketchpad to display and manipulate mathematical objects to answer questions that arose in the course of a presentation. The slides he created before and during such presentations were archived so that interested students could review the material at a later date. Numerous participants reported developing similar technological skills in their prior work and using these skills to help organize and execute their work as teachers.

Participants also reported that they had become clear communicators and adept presenters from working in careers that involved interacting with colleagues, administrators, and clients. Having grown accustomed to making both formal and informal presentations to a variety of audiences, participants had little trouble feeling confident while leading a class, being observed by an administrator, or dealing with contentious parents. Thus, participants not only brought with them skills as presenters and communicators, they brought the confidence associated with having applied these skills in competitive, demanding settings. Participants appeared to be well served by the skills themselves, as well as by the confidence to practice these skills in their schools.

Nearly all participants reported that, in their former work, accomplishing organizational objectives well required extensive interaction between individuals within and outside their organizations. For example, Carter, a former midlevel manager in the software industry, explained how his work involved interactions in three general directions within his organization: (1) "left and right," or with managers in other departments to synchronize the timing of their work and to ensure that departmental objectives were aligned with organizational goals; (2) "downward," to explain work tasks to the developers that worked within his department; and (3) "upward," with senior administrators to inform them of his department's progress.

While most of Carter's "downward" interactions were informal, the "upward" progress reports to senior managers often entailed formal presentations. Carter illustrated the importance of interaction between colleagues in the software industry when he remarked, "My God, if people couldn't work together, these businesses would have fallen apart."

In addition to making presentations to colleagues and superiors within their organizations, some participants were required to interact with, and make presentations to, audiences outside of their organizations. For example, Marcia's work as a sales support engineer involved presenting her company's software to prospective clients. Senior managers at Kerry's management consulting firm would often make impromptu demands in front of clients that she present overviews of her team's work. The culmination of much of Joe's work as a telecommunications engineer was the testimony he presented at state and federal hearings.

Participants reported that their interactive former careers had made them clear communicators and adept presenters—skills that they claimed enabled them to feel confident at the head of the classroom and in their interactions with their students, students' parents, and administrators. For example, Kerry's practice making impromptu presentations in front of clients had left her confident in her "ability to think on [her] feet." As a result, she did not feel like "a stuttering nightmare" in her first year of teaching. "I just didn't feel overwhelmed," she recalled, "I felt more confident. I had already done all that." Similarly, Marcia's experience presenting her company's software to senior executives taught her how to interact with the high-powered parents in her suburban school district. She noted:

> I think I've had less trouble dealing with parents than I would have if I hadn't spent 10 years [in my former career]. I learned how to talk to people at different levels of an organization, and that's been very useful. So if somebody comes in here and they're vice president of a Fortune 500 company, I'm not particularly intimidated. I'm not a pushover and that's pretty clear, so [the parents] don't typically mess with me. I think that comes from being a midcareer entrant. Having that confidence in myself as I came in [to teaching] was a huge asset.

Two participants, Peg and Joe, reported that their familiarity with securing external grants in their former careers was valuable in their new work as teachers. For instance, as a teacher, Joe received a grant to equip several classrooms with LCD projectors, which were used to display presentations that teachers created with software like Geometry Sketchpad. He was in the process of applying for another grant that would equip five classrooms with tablet computers and wireless routers that would further aid such presentations. Joe believed that his technological savvy was a capability that distinguished him from his colleagues. "Everyone's giving away lots of money," he acknowledged. "You just have to know where it is . . . as far as other teachers getting grants, at least in the math department, I don't know if anyone [else] has."

TO WHAT EXTENT DID SCHOOLS CAPITALIZE ON PARTICIPANTS' SKILLS? WHICH SCHOOL CHARACTERISTICS AFFECTED PARTICIPANTS' ABILITY TO SHARE THEIR STRENGTHS WITH THEIR COLLEAGUES AND SUPERIORS?

While nearly all participants reported that their knowledge and skills informed their teaching and their interactions with students and students' parents, few reported having opportunities where they and their colleagues could share their respective strengths. Unlike their former careers, in which there was much interaction, they performed the central task of their work as teachers—classroom instruction—independently. Although there were occasionally opportunities for participants to interact with colleagues before and after instruction took place, these interactions were typically brief and informal.

Further, the physical and administrative structures of participants' schools, as well as their schools' limited technological infrastructures, reinforced the teachers' isolation. Taken together, the isolated nature of teaching and the cellular organization of participants' schools (Lortie, 1975) meant that participants and their colleagues had few opportunities to share their respective knowledge and skills. Thus, many participants reported feeling that their schools had not capitalized on their skills and that many of their talents remained untapped.

Participants reported having limited contact with anyone other than the students in their classrooms, corroborating a long history of literature that describes the isolated nature of teaching (e.g., McLaughlin & Talbert, 2001; Johnson, 1990; Goodlad, 1984; Lortie, 1975). Nearly all participants described having far fewer interactions with colleagues in teaching than they had had with their coworkers in their former workplace.[2] Tim spoke for many participants when he reported, "There's very little, if any, collaboration here. There was a lot more collaboration in industry than there is here. I was more a part of a team at [my consulting firm].

Here, it's kind of like you've got 180 people all doing their own thing." Kate echoed Tim's sentiments when she remarked, "I had a lot of interaction [in my former job in finance]. I came here and I was very isolated in my classroom." Roy explained that there were no organizational tasks in teaching that intertwined colleagues' work:

> Teaching is much more of a loner's operation, even in this place where there's a lot of collaboration . . . it's still you in front of that class, it's still you grading that pile of tests, it's still you making [the tests] up, it's still you deciding what to do about the fact that your kids didn't do very well on that exam, it's still you dealing with the cheating in your classroom. There's not a real opportunity for collaboration in the way that we collaborate in industry.

That Roy found teaching more of a "loner's operation" than software programming is notable, as Roy's portrayal of programming suggested that his work involved *more* independent tasks than the jobs of many in the sample.

In teaching, because organizational tasks and outcomes did not require colleagues to collaborate, most interactions were brief, informal, and optional. Participants reported that the majority of their interaction with peers occurred impromptu during lunch periods. Occasionally, these interactions addressed subject-related topics and sparked stimulating conversations between departmental colleagues. More often, they were opportunities to chat informally, share resources (such as a review sheet or quiz), or exchange last-minute tips on how to introduce a topic. While participants valued these interactions, the interactions were clearly not substantive enough to change participants' sentiment that teaching was isolating work.

Formal opportunities to interact with colleagues, such as during department meetings, afforded equally few opportunities for participants and their colleagues to share their knowledge and skills. Formal faculty meetings were infrequent and brief and were usually spent addressing pressing departmental issues, such as developing common student assessments or deciding which texts to use. Kate said that department meetings were usually opportunities to "make finals, midterms, develop curriculum guidelines [to accompany new texts], plan the department math fair . . . things like that." Given the infrequency of formal meetings and the need to address pressing issues during them, opportunities to discuss instruction were rare. Jerry explained:

> We have begged, borrowed, and stolen time during the course of the year to get together with other teachers who are working on the same subject before big exams and say, "We're at this point here, you need to be at this point before the final exam or the midterm exam." We *might* (Jerry's emphasis) get to talk about certain things that we're doing in the classroom, but those times are very, very few and far between. I'd like to see them happen more often.

Had there been more time in these formal meetings, and had the meetings been focused on matters pertaining to teaching and learning, Jerry and his colleagues might have been able to discuss the benefits of using practical classroom exercises rather than those available in their texts. Similarly, Marcia might have presented a compelling case for using the graphing calculator in conjunction with certain lessons. No participants described having such opportunities during formal meetings.

Just as participants brought valuable knowledge, skills, and resources to teaching, their colleagues possessed a wealth of instructional experience that might have informed these participants' efforts in the classroom. Participants were unanimous in their portrayals of colleagues as being knowledgeable of their craft and generous in sharing materials and resources. However, the isolated nature of teaching meant that participants had few opportunities to glean in-depth information on the finer points of teaching from their experienced colleagues.

Participants reported that the organization of their schools reinforced the isolation in which they worked. Three of the schools in this study were organized by traditional, subject-area departments. One was further subdivided into grade-level houses. The fourth school in the sample was divided into small-school units that were composed of teachers from all subject disciplines. None of these organizational structures seemed to promote meaningful interactions among teachers.

The small-school organizational structure allowed teachers to monitor student progress and exchange ideas about, in Tim's words, "basic pedagogical things like classroom management." However, it did not provide opportunities for participants to engage in the kinds of subject-related discussions that might have showcased, for example, their practical understanding of their subjects. Jerry concurred with Tim, reporting that his school's small-school structure afforded only minimal opportunities to work on subject-related tasks:

> [The small-school structure] inhibits [the interaction I'd like to have with my math-teacher colleagues]. . . . It's good to have the cross-curriculum thing where you're meeting with history and English and science teachers, but I'd like to have more opportunities to meet with math teachers. In a lot of ways I feel like I'm working in a void.

The math coordinator at Jerry's school had deemed the isolation among math teachers so limiting that he succeeded in getting an external grant to compensate math teachers for participating in professional development outside of the school day. About one-third of the department attended these meetings, including the three teachers from this school who participated in this study: Jerry, Tim, and Carter. Had it not been for this grant, Tim doubted that he would know the names of half his math department colleagues—this after four years of full-time employment.

Jerry, Tim, and Carter all imagined that a departmental organization would be more conducive for discussing instruction and subject-related topics. Interestingly, participants who were organized into traditional departments also described having few opportunities to engage in such discussions. Similarly, while participants in traditionally organized schools were not forced to meet with departmental colleagues outside of the school day, formal departmental meetings were still devoted to taking care of basic requirements, such as developing common assessments.

The grade-level houses that complemented the departments at Shelly and Kerry's school did little to promote interactions among teachers. Shelly described the purpose of the houses as being to "distribute paperwork . . . there's not a whole lot of collaboration that goes on."

The physical layouts of participants' schools also limited the extent to which participants and their colleagues were able to exchange their respective strengths. Few schools had common rooms where members of the same organizational unit (i.e., department or small school) could meet, meaning that many participants remained in their "egg-crate" classrooms for much of the day (Lortie, 1975). In Kate's case, the classroom she was assigned in her first year of teaching was at the opposite end of the building from where the math department classrooms were located. Kate's physical location made it virtually impossible to exchange ideas and resources with departmental colleagues during the short periods between classes. It wasn't until her room was relocated that Kate even had the opportunity to meet many of the teachers within her department. In Kate's former workplace, by contrast, cubicle suites enabled a relatively effortless flow of information between team members and across departments.

Roy and Marcia's school, which was organized into subject departments, appeared to have the physical layout most conducive for promoting interaction among teachers. About three-fourths of the math teachers had desks in one of two departmental offices where they could work during free periods or before or after school; the remaining department members worked in their own classrooms. While Roy, whose desk was in the larger of the two offices, saw benefits to this physical arrangement, they did not outweigh his general sense of isolation. Roy explained:

> This [physical arrangement] is done on purpose to try [to] provide more chances for us to be able to talk. And in fact, we do. We can just turn around and ask somebody a question: "I haven't done this before. Could you help me? How do you teach this?" There's a lot of that kind of stuff going on. Whereas, if we each

had our individual rooms, it'd be much harder to get that to happen. So this is a department where the ethos of the department is collaboration and sharing and helping each other, and it's organized to do that, and people, in fact, carry that out. And yet it still feels to me like a loner's job.

The physical structure of Roy's school may not have changed his sentiments about the isolated nature of teachers' work; however, he was one of the few participants to describe engaging in the kinds of interactions that might allow him and his colleagues to share their respective knowledge and skills, underscoring the importance of a school's physical layout in this regard.

Participants' former work sites, in addition to having effective physical layouts, had technological infrastructures that facilitated the kinds of interaction that their jobs required. These infrastructures allowed participants to communicate with colleagues on their teams, as well as with those in other departments or geographic locations. In addition, centralized databases and intranets allowed coworkers to organize, archive, and share resources, such as reports that had been presented to prior clients. In several cases, participants' former organizations had developed their own networks—prior to the creation of the Internet—to enable the efficient exchange of information between employees throughout the country.

Other participants described technological infrastructures that allowed employees to access centralized databases of materials (reports, contracts, etc.) as well as folders where they could organize, archive, and share work that needed to be integrated. At the software company where one participant had worked, employees held virtual meetings or online discussions when their work required performing tasks, such as brainstorming, that were suited for online forums.

Some participants, like Marcia and Joe, described having access to technology that helped them to organize and carry out their work in the classroom. However, no participants described having access in their schools to technology, outside of email clients, that facilitated interaction among colleagues. Carter explained:

We have no technology that allows [us to interact with other teachers]. There are four or five PCs that are able to access the network, but they're old technology, they're very slow. There are one or two printers that sometimes work, but which most recently have not been working. And there's very little paper . . . it's ridiculous. There's definitely nothing like a computer on every desk where you could put your lesson plans and share them with other teachers in a newsroom type setting. Not only do we not have the capability of doing that, we don't have the vision to do it, which is even more serious.

Carter saw great promise in the use of technology in education were schools able to secure the resources. "Imagine a case," he noted enthusiastically, "where you bring in a new teacher and you can share lesson plans and handouts in electronic form, and you have a printer in your own room and can just print them off. . . . "

Several participants reported that the lack of technological resources at their schools also made it difficult to apply the technological skills they brought from their former careers toward constructive ends. For instance, Kate reported that the lack of resources in her classroom, and the difficulty of gaining access to the school's computer lab, meant that her technological skills were gradually slipping. "I'm definitely losing my skills," she lamented, "technology is one thing that I'm losing over time here."

CONCLUSIONS AND IMPLICATIONS

Several findings from this investigation are important for tomorrow's leaders to note. First, many math and science midcareer entrants bring skills and knowledge—subject related and otherwise—from their former careers that ease their transition into teaching and that have the potential to influence important student outcomes. From their prior careers, many participants gained valuable, practical experience performing the mathematical and scientific processes they are now teaching.

Even those whose former work did not entail extensive application of their subject areas reported developing the analytic thinking skills that undergird their subjects. Participants also brought a familiarity with technology, communication, and presentation skills, and grant-writing capabilities to their schools, which further supported their work and brought resources to their schools.

While more research is needed to understand whether and how midcareer entrants influence the way their schools operate, the math and science midcareer entrants in this study certainly brought skills and knowledge that have the potential to transform schools in several important ways. For instance, in responding to this knowledge base (Cooper & Conley, this volume), these findings suggest that administrators could look to math and science midcareer entrants to provide technological consultation to their schools to expand and renew the technological professional development of the school site.

Midcareer entrants represent changing resources available to schools; they are well poised to help respond to the changing environment in which schools and districts now operate. Similarly, midcareer entrants with experience restructuring organizations might be able to provide invaluable counsel about streamlining organizational efficiency—a rather urgent priority given the budgetary restrictions facing many communities. Lastly, midcareer entrants' ease in their social interactions with colleagues, administrators, and parents suggests managerial competence and political wherewithal that could help administrators accomplish organizational objectives. Further, midcareer entrants' experience performing interactive work in highly collaborative organizations may make them logical candidates for administrative or managerial roles within schools or districts.

The encouraging findings about midcareer entrants' potential are tempered by participants' revelations about the limited extent to which their schools have capitalized on their skills to date. Clearly, tomorrow's leaders would do well to invest more time and energy into identifying midcareer entrants' strengths, as well as strategies for using these strengths to improve the operation of their schools.

Further, administrators must take the lead in reforming the organizational characteristics that impede collaboration. While math and science midcareer entrants may bring the experience and ability to work collaboratively with their peers, they are unlikely to tackle the reform of organizational norms and physical structures on their own. Future leaders will need to think creatively about how to reshape schools—physically, virtually, or both—to provide midcareer entrants and their colleagues more opportunities to share their respective strengths. Given math and science midcareer entrants' familiarity with technology, they may be well suited to offer advice on the design and implementation of technological infrastructures that can help overcome the limitations of many schools' physical facilities.

This study also has important implications for the design of school-based teacher induction and professional development programs. To date, many district and building administrators have taken a *one-size-fits-all* approach to induction. While some districts offer differentiated programs for teachers who are new to the profession, as opposed to experienced teachers who are new to their school, few have analyzed how mid- and first-career entrants' needs may differ.

The evidence presented here suggests, for example, that midcareer entrants may need less support than first-career entrants with exercises intended to bolster confidence and composure in preparation for back-to-school nights or parent-teacher conferences.

Tomorrow's leaders should also investigate whether the most effective mid- and first-career entrants in their buildings desire similar or different opportunities to retain their interest throughout their careers. Because midcareer teachers enter the profession with years of professional experience, they may desire opportunities to contribute to school initiatives that draw on the skills and knowledge that they honed in their former career. Even midcareer entrants who left their former careers out of disinterest or dissatisfaction may seek to apply the skills that they acquired to their new work as teachers. First-career entrants, by comparison, may be inclined to leave teaching after several years on the job unless they have opportunities to enhance their subject knowledge or develop additional skills by participating in related work outside the field of teaching. While half- or full-year sabbaticals[3] are not typical in K-12 public schools, administrators may find that such opportunities help retain effective teachers who would have otherwise left the field.

In summary, midcareer entrants' increasing presence in the teacher workforce presents future leaders with both an opportunity and a challenge. In the years to come, part of what will define the most successful building and district administrators is their ability to create schools that attract both talented mid- and first-career entrants, capitalize on their respective strengths, and provide each subgroup with the supports and opportunities needed to promote their respective professional growth.

NOTES

1. Broughman and Rollefson (2000) identify a "delayed entrant" as "a first-year teacher who had engaged in other activities in the year or years between graduating from college or receiving his or her highest degree and becoming a teacher."

2. Shelly, the former lab researcher, was the only participant whose previous career seemed to involve a similar level of interdependence and independence as teaching. Marcia's career in technical sales support hadn't involved interacting with many colleagues, but the frequent contact she had with clients made the work feel interactive. All other participants portrayed their former work as notably more interactive than their work as teachers.

3. Few schools have the resources to make partially or fully subsidized sabbaticals for teachers possible. However, if schools were better equipped to help teachers secure external funding for such ventures, teachers might be willing to commit to returning to their schools for at least a specified minimum term after the sabbatical.

REFERENCES

American Competitiveness Initiative. (2006). Retrieved January 18, 2008, from www.whitehouse.gov/stateoftheunion/2006/aci/index.html#section6.

Broughman, S. P., & Rollefson, M. R. (2000). *Teacher Supply in the United States: Sources of Newly Hired Teachers in Public and Private Schools, 1987–88, 1993–94* (NCES 2000–309). Washington, D.C.: National Center for Education Statistics.

Chin, E., Young, J., & Floyd, B. (2004). *Placing beginning teachers in hard-to-staff schools: Dilemmas posed by alternative certification programs.* Chicago: American Association of Colleges of Teacher Education.

Crow, G. M., Levine, L, & Nager, N. (1990). No more business as usual: Career changers who become teachers. *American Journal of Education, 98*(3), May 1990, 197–223.

Dee, T. (2004). The Race Connection. *Education Next, 4*(2), 53–59.

Dee, T. (2005). A teacher like me: Does race, ethnicity, or gender matter? *American Economic Review, 95*(2), 158–165.

Dee, T. (2006). The why chromosome: How a teacher's gender affects boys and girls, *Education Next, 6*(4), 68–75.

Feistritzer, C. E. (1999). *The making of a teacher: A report on teacher preparation in the U.S.* Washington, D.C.: National Center for Education Information.

Feistritzer, C. E. (2005). *Alternative certification: A state-by-state analysis.* Washington, D.C.: National Center for Education Information.

Goodlad, J. I. (1984). *A place called school.* New York: McGraw-Hill.

Grant, G., & Murray, C. (1999). *Teaching in America: The slow revolution.* Cambridge, MA: Harvard University Press.

Johnson, S. M. (1990). *Teachers at work.* New York: Basic Books.

Johnson, S. M., Birkeland, S. E., Donaldson, M. L., Kardos, S. M., Kauffman, D., Liu, E., & Peske, H. G. (2004). *Finders and Keepers: Helping new teachers survive and thrive in our schools.* San Francisco, CA: Jossey-Bass.

Johnson, S. M., Birkeland, S., & Peske, H. (2005). *A difficult balance: Incentives and quality control in alternative certification programs.* A report published by The Project on the Next Generation of Teachers.

McLaughlin, M. W., & Talbert, J. E. (2001). *Professional communities and the work of high school teaching.* Chicago: The University of Chicago Press.

Murnane, R., Singer, J., Willett, J., Kemple, J., & Olsen, R. (Eds.). (1991). *Who will teach? Policies that matter.* Cambridge, MA: Harvard University Press.

National Academies Press. (2000). *Attracting science and mathematics Ph.D.s to secondary school education.* Washington, D.C.: Author.

National Academies Press. (2005). *Rising above the gathering storm: Energizing and employing America for a brighter economic future.* Washington, D.C.: Author.

National Commission on Mathematics and Science Teaching for the 21st Century (NCMST). (2000). *Before it's too late.* Retrieved January 18, 2008, from www.ed.gov/inits/Math/glenn/report.pdf.

Natriello, G., & Zumwalt, K. (1992). Challenges to an alternative route for teacher education. In A. Lieberman (Ed.) *The changing contexts of teaching: Ninety-first yearbook of the National Society for the Study of Education* (pp. 59–78). Chicago: University of Chicago Press.

Natriello, G., & Zumwalt, K. (1993). New teachers for urban schools: The contribution of the provisional teacher program in New Jersey. *Education and Urban Society, 26*(1), 49–62.

Novak, D., & Knowles, G. (1992). *Life Histories and the Transition to Teaching as a Second Career.* Unpublished paper presented to the Annual Meeting of the American Educational Research Association. San Francisco, CA.

Ruenzel, D. (2002). Tortuous routes. *Education Next,* Spring, 42–49.

Rury, J. L. (1989). Who became teachers?: The social characteristics of teachers in American history. In D. Warren (Ed.), *American teachers: Histories of a profession at work* (pp. 7–48). New York: Macmillan.

Shen, J. (1997). Has the alternative certification policy materialized its promise? A comparison between traditionally and alternatively certified teachers in public schools. *Educational Evaluation and Policy Analysis, 19*(3), 276–283.

Shen, J. (1998). Alternative certification, minority teachers, and urban education. *Education and Urban Society, 31*(1), 30–41.

Spencer, D. A. (2001). Teachers' work in historical and social context. In V. Richardson (Ed.), *Handbook of research on teaching* (4th ed., pp. 803–825). Washington, D.C.: American Educational Research Association.

Steele, C. M. (1997). A threat in the air: How stereotypes shape intellectual identity and performance. *American Psychologist, 52*(6), 613–629.

Strizek, G. A., Pittsonberger, J. L., Riordan, K. E., Lyter, D. M., & Orlofsky, G. F. (2006). Characteristics of schools, districts, teachers, principals, and school libraries in the United States: 2003–2004 Schools and Staffing Survey (NCES 2006-313 Revised). U.S. Department of Education, National Center for Educational Statistics. Washington, D.C.: U. S. Government Printing Office.

Tift, S. (1989). The lure of the classroom. *Time, 133*(7), 69.

Wiggan, G. (2007). Race, school achievement and educational inequality: Toward a student-based inquiry perspective. *Review of Educational Research, 77*(3), 310–333.

Chapter Five

New Principal Isolation and Efficacy[1]

Scott C. Bauer and S. David Brazer

New principals enter into their positions with the expectations and aspirations of their school communities on their shoulders. At a minimum, they are often seen as a breath of fresh air and a source of new ideas; quite often, a change in leadership brings with it an aura of hope. More important, principals' leadership generally is seen as having a strong influence on student learning (Leithwood, Louis, Anderson, & Wahlstrom, 2004; Waters, Marzano, & McNulty, 2003). Consequently, schools and districts may depend on their new principals to lead the school community to improve student achievement substantially.

Such attribution may easily morph into the somewhat risky notion of a "turnaround" principal who will make all the difference in a struggling school. Whether new principals can help fulfill such dreams depends largely on the skills, knowledge, and dispositions they bring into their jobs. Doubtless, frustrations occur along the way, but how new principals cope with and respond to those frustrations is critical to their long-term success.

One factor that may enhance new principals' probability of success is what Leithwood and Jantzi (2008) describe as principals' beliefs about their self-efficacy, or leader self-efficacy. They find that principals with high degrees of self-efficacy—that is, their beliefs about their ability to achieve goals—display behaviors linked to improved student achievement. That principals are explicitly and implicitly rewarded for better student performance heightens the import of this factor in the work lives of the principals themselves. Related research investigating new principals' work emphasizes the importance of isolation as an influence on outcomes such as burnout (Stephenson & Bauer, forthcoming) and job satisfaction (Bauer, Brazer, & Stephenson, submitted).

This chapter adds another piece to the puzzle relating to factors that influence outcomes reflecting the quality of new principals' work lives and, by extension, their potential for success, by exploring the relationships among factors reflecting the working conditions of new principals, their perception of isolation, and their sense of self-efficacy. We argue that self-efficacy is an important outcome often influenced by school districts. New principals have common experiences that exacerbate their sense of isolation.

Purpose

The purpose of this research is to demonstrate how role ambiguity, role conflict, role overload, social support, and involvement in a coaching program affect new principals' isolation and self-efficacy beliefs. More specifically, we wish to learn if isolation mediates the independent variables' influence on self-efficacy. Stated another way, we wanted to know whether the effect of the independent variables operates according to the following pattern: independent variables (e.g., role ambiguity) → isolation → self-efficacy.

In previous work as cited above, we found that isolation has this effect, partially mediating the influence of role ambiguity and fully mediating the impact of social support on new principals' job satisfaction and some manifestations of burnout. Here, we further test the importance of the role of isolation in influencing work outcomes experienced by new principals by exploring its relationship to a different dependent variable, self-efficacy.

Significance

The importance of the link between principals' self-efficacy and job performance is gradually becoming more clearly established (Goddard, Woolfolk Hoy, & Hoy, 2004; Leithwood & Jantzi, 2008; Tschannen-Moran & Gareis, 2004). The strength of the theoretical and empirical work that has taken place over the past 30 years on the subject of self-efficacy (Bandura, 1977, 1997) and the interest that it has generated in teacher self-efficacy and collective efficacy (e.g., Gibson & Dembo, 1984; Guskey & Passaro, 1994; Hoy, Sweetland, & Smith, 2002) suggests that self-efficacy is a concept that may help to clarify why principals—and in the case of this particular study, new principals—vary in their degree of success.

Unfortunately, principal self-efficacy has been rarely studied (Tschannen-Moran & Gareis, 2004). Less clear than how principals perceive their ability to achieve their own goals is the influence that district factors might have on their beliefs (Leithwood & Jantzi, 2008). By exploring the relationships among specific work-related independent variables and self-efficacy, this study addresses both a theoretical and practical need.

With respect to theory, establishing the relationships among factors such as role stress, social support and coaching, as independent variables; isolation; and self-efficacy is of great value to our thinking about the induction process for new principals. If self-efficacy is as important to job performance generally and teacher performance specifically as the literature suggests, then it seems critical to conceptualize the role self-efficacy plays in new principal performance.

We are not ready to reach that far in this chapter, however, because we do not yet understand how self-efficacy is enhanced or diminished as a result of how new principals experience their jobs. Our elaboration of a model that encompasses working conditions, isolation, and self-efficacy helps to open the door to future research on the relationship between new principal self-efficacy and measures of their job performance. Such a link is critical if we are to understand at least one component in how effective principals develop.

Our professional experience, stories from graduates of our education leadership program, and research suggest that new principals are not always adequately supported by the school districts that employ them. This is not to say that districts don't try, but sometimes their efforts can be received differently by principals from what was originally intended.

Better specification of and empirical support for a model of new principal self-efficacy hold promise for guiding school districts in more effective job induction and ongoing professional development for new principals. In short, if we want new principals to do their jobs well, we need to understand how to enhance precursors to success such as a leader's sense of self-efficacy.

Research Questions

The research questions for this study focus on investigating the predictive relationship between measures relating to the work experience of new principals, reported levels of isolation, and their sense of self-efficacy. We employ a three-step analytic process (Baron & Kenney, 1986) that is informed by the following questions:

1) What part do role ambiguity, role overload, role conflict, social support, and participation in a formal coaching program play in predicting new principals' sense of isolation?
2) What part do role ambiguity, role overload, role conflict, social support, and participation in a formal coaching program play in predicting new principals' perceptions related to self-efficacy?
3) How is the influence of the independent variables of role ambiguity, role overload, role conflict, social support, and participation in a formal coaching program on self-efficacy mediated through perceived isolation?

Answers to these questions are organized by the way in which we conceptualize the development of new principals' sense of self-efficacy. The conceptual framework that follows below explains the perspective we take on how the independent and dependent variables relate to one another.

REVIEW OF LITERATURE AND CONCEPTUAL FRAMEWORK

The existing literature supports the use of role ambiguity, role conflict, role overload, social support, and participation in a coaching program as predictors of the quality of a new principal's work experience. Our hypothesis that isolation serves as a mediator of the relationship between these predictors and the outcome of self-efficacy is supported theoretically by the relevant literature on isolation and the other study variables.

Very little debate exists about the fact that isolation has a negative impact on the quality of the work experience of teachers (Cookson, 2005; Garmston, 2007; Hord, 2007; Schlechte, Yssel, & Merbler, 2005). The literature shows a long history of isolation among education professionals, stemming primarily from the nature of classrooms and the manner in which they are spatially grouped throughout school buildings (Glickman, Gordon, & Ross-Gordon, 2004; Dreeben, 1973). Teacher isolation and, by extension, principal isolation, functions as a complex variable that affects work outcomes such as efficacy and is influenced by workplace characteristics.

We suggest that principal isolation is more than an outcome of the work environment, influencing how principals, particularly new principals, process and respond to factors in their work environment. Consequently, we position isolation as acting in concert with other variables to affect new principals' self-efficacy beliefs. Specifically, new principals' sense of self-efficacy will result from a combination of their perceptions of role ambiguity, role overload, role conflict, social support, and participation in a formal coaching program; these variables influence isolation, which in turn influences self-efficacy. All six are explained in more detail below.

Principal Isolation

Professional isolation is embedded in the legacy of how the principalship developed. The administrative demands of schooling have changed drastically since the days of the one-room schoolhouse, most recently influenced by increasing diversity among students, waning public confidence in schools, and pressure on schools and school districts to improve test scores under high-stakes accountability policies. Schools have moved from having no principal, to being loosely led by "principal teachers," to having principals that must take full responsibility for all of the administrative and instructional imperatives of complex organizations (Cuban, 1988).

The trend through all of the changes in the principalship that remains common is principals' tendency to have sole responsibility for school outcomes and the strong possibility that they will make many of their key decisions alone.

Research on the topic of principal isolation, though, is relatively sparse (Norton, 2001; Robbins & Alvey, 2003; Schlechte, Yssel, & Merbler, 2005). Howard and Mallory's (2008) work supports the inclusion of isolation as a variable that operates in concert with the stress created by principal job expectations in the form of role stress. Dussault and Thibideau's (1997) research extends the examination of isolation as having an effect on the quality of work outcomes such as job satisfaction or self-efficacy. A more recent study conducted by Izgar (2009) shows a statistical relationship between measures of principal loneliness and depression. The research reported in this chapter helps to consolidate and confirm past research related to the import of principal isolation.

Role Stress

The three subcategories of role stress (i.e., ambiguity, conflict, and overload) function as organizational attributes that contribute to outcomes reflecting the quality of the work experience for professionals such as school principals (Bunnell, 2006; Conley, Muncey, & You, 2006; Wong, DeSanctis, & Staudenmayer, 2007). These variables also serve as important indicators of the organizational design of schools and, we believe, have particular relevance for the study of new principals. For example, demands on principals to perform as instructional leaders make their work more complex and lead to a much greater likelihood that they will experience role ambiguity, conflict, or overload on a regular basis, particularly when new to the job (Norton, 2003).

Thus the subcategories of role stress are reasonable predictors of the quality of the work experience for new principals. Role ambiguity, role conflict, and job overload, we hypothesize, are important negative influences on self-efficacy because they lower new principals' sense of their success in the position and they may mute positive feedback. The link between job stress and depression noted above clearly suggests that new principals' anxiety, an important affective contributor to self-efficacy (Goddard, Woolfolk Hoy, & Hoy, 2004), would be heightened.

Social Support

Research on teachers and professionals in other fields shows that the creation of informal social networks in the workplace—that provide support mechanisms, such as reassurance of worth and guidance—can reduce stress for individuals who work in contexts and settings, such as the principalship, that tend to isolate employees (Brook, Sawyer, & Rimm-Kaufman, 2007; Marshall, Michaels, & Mulki, 2007). Social support in this study represents the extent to which new principals experience guidance and receive needed resources from other professionals within the work environment.

This kind of social support may come from both informal networks and formal programs established for the expressed purpose of helping new principals to adjust to the demands of their jobs. Social support has great potential to provide positive models of success that might enhance a new principal's sense of self-efficacy (Goddard, Woolfolk Hoy, & Hoy, 2004).

It is not a foregone conclusion that social support efforts reduce isolation; rather, the effect of social support on isolation depends on two factors: (1) the nature of the support itself, which could be structural (some sort of formal program), social, or a combination of the two; and (2) how support is perceived and received by the new principal. In the context of this study, social support refers primarily to the mechanisms or opportunities in place to promote a sense of connectedness; isolation, in contrast, relates to an emotional or affective state of the new principal—that is, feelings of loneliness or disconnectedness. The existing evidence, coupled with the lack of guidance about the influence these two variables have on specific outcomes such as self-efficacy, supports the concept of analyzing social support as a separate and distinct variable from professional isolation, and as a predictor of self-efficacy for the study of new principals.

Coaching

Coaching, in this study, represents the formal structures that an employer puts in place to ensure an individual has the skills he or she needs to be productive. Employers use coaching programs to reduce negative factors such as job dissatisfaction in the work environment and to improve employee retention (Herrington, Herrington, Kervin, & Ferry, 2006; Hobson & Sharp, 2005).

Because different kinds of coaching programs tend to be treated as interventions—designed to improve the performance of new principals—and because participation in such programs is designed to enhance participants' skills and to help them build a network of peers from whom they can learn—based in part on models of past principal success—this study treats coaching as a contributor to self-efficacy beliefs, and one that may also affect the degree of perceived isolation.

Self-Efficacy

Self-efficacy is, at its core, a person's belief about his or her ability to complete a task successfully, and it predicts the likelihood of persistence through difficult circumstances (Bandura, 1997). In education, the study of self-efficacy has focused mostly on classroom teachers, with the result that higher levels of student achievement are associated with higher degrees of teacher self-efficacy and collective efficacy (Goddard, Woolfolk Hoy, & Hoy, 2004).

Leithwood and Jantzi (2008) have also found that higher degrees of principals' self-efficacy and perceptions of their schools' collective efficacy are associated with enhanced school improvement. Furthermore, principals' self-efficacy is malleable and susceptible to district influences. Important though these findings are, they do not deal with the links among factors such as role stress, social support, or coaching; isolation; and self-efficacy, nor does this research focus on the work experience of new principals. At this point, we propose a somewhat novel model for new principals' experiences.

Conceptual Framework

In the framework established for this study, role stress (subdivided into ambiguity, conflict, and overload), social support, and coaching all serve as predictors of the new principals' sense of self-efficacy. Isolation for new principals functions as a mediator that both predicts self-efficacy and impacts the manner in which the other variables predict these outcomes. We hypothesize that new principals are especially vulnerable to role stress and isolation by virtue of their inexperience. Consequently, they are at high risk for depressed levels of self-efficacy. Figure 5.1 provides a visual representation of this framework.

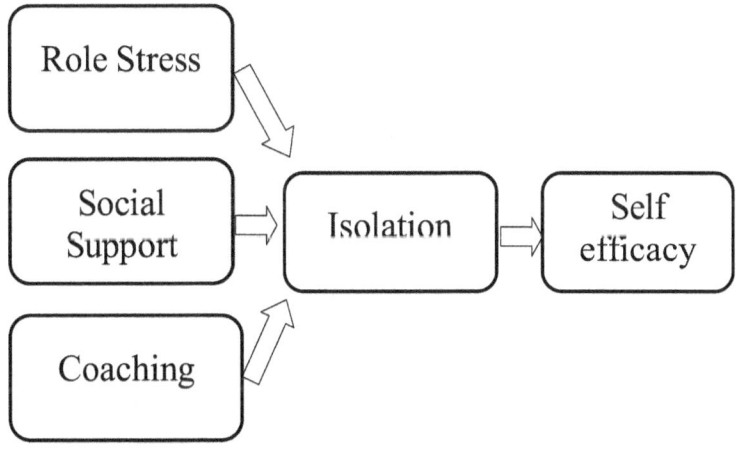

Figure 5.1. Conceptual Framework

METHODS

Participants and Setting

This study uses survey data collected from a sample of first-year school principals from Louisiana. The data were collected as part of a three-year longitudinal study, examining the impact of instructional coaching on new principals. Two groups of principals were selected for inclusion, based on their experience level (all of them were first-year principals) and their willingness to participate in the study as either a member of a treatment or comparison group.

The first group participated in a federally supported grant that involved designing and implementing a highly structured coaching and mentoring program for new principals. The second group comprised all remaining new principals in the state, and this group served as a comparison or control group.

The treatment group consisted of all new principals in participating school systems. Of the 86 principals in this group, 82 consented to participate (95% response rate). Of the 187 principals who made up the comparison group from the remaining jurisdictions, 121 principals elected to participate (65% response rate). For this study, a subset of the data from the three-year project was used, including surveys completed by first-year principals during their initial year of involvement in the project (n = 203).

School and Principal Demographics

The principals in the two groups serve in a variety of demographically different communities, ranging from rural to suburban to urban. The demographic characteristics of the principals surveyed represent a wide range of backgrounds: Male principals number 58 or 29% of the total sample. Female principals include 143 or 70% of the overall number of participants. (Two principals did not report gender or ethnicity data.) African-American principals make up 67 or 33% of the total; Hispanic principals 3 or 2%; white/non-Hispanic 129 or 64%; and multiethnic 2 or 1% of participants.

Of the 203 participants, 122 (60%) are principals of elementary schools; 36 (18%) serve in middle and junior high schools; 29 (14%) are principals in high schools; and the remainder (16 or 8%) come from schools with other grade configurations (e.g., K-12).

Measures

Five survey scales and one treatment group designation provide the data for this study. Each measures one of the major study variables: role stress, social support, coaching, isolation, and self-efficacy (see Appendix 5.1).

Role Stress Measures

This study utilizes survey items first developed by Rizzo, House, and Lirtzman (1970) to measure perceptions of role conflict and ambiguity within large organizations. The 17-item instrument used here was first developed by Bacharach and Aiken (1976) and was used in Conley, Bacharach, and Bauer (1989) in school settings. The instrument measures three categories of role stress: ambiguity (four items), conflict (seven items), and overload (six items).

Participants are asked to evaluate each item using a five-point Likert scale with the response options of "strongly disagree," "disagree," "neutral," "agree," and "strongly agree," with a score of 1 representing the lowest, and 5 representing the highest degree of role stress. Higher levels of role stress, in general, are thought to reflect a less desirable work condition for respondents (i.e., higher levels of role ambiguity, conflict, and overload reflect a more negative assessment of the quality of work life).

Items intended to measure role ambiguity focus on aspects of the new principal's job that are confusing or unclear, like the item "I feel certain about how much authority I have" (an item that is reverse-scored in the four-item scale). Items intended to measure role conflict deal with aspects of the new principal's role that force the participant to deal with competing conditions and/or expectations, like "I work with two or more groups who operate quite differently." Those intended to measure overload focus on parts of the responsibilities of the principal that may lead to feelings of being overwhelmed, like the item "I cannot ever seem to catch up."

Social Support

The Social Provisions Scale (Cutrona & Russell, 1987; 1990) has been used to measure the six social provisions suggested by Weiss (1974). This study uses four of these provisions, selected because of their importance in relation to the implementation of the coaching process: reassurance of worth, reliable alliance, guidance, and opportunity for nurturance. Participants are asked to respond to each of sixteen items with the choice that best reflects their feelings about relationships at work, using the five-point Likert scale previously described.

Examples of positive items include "There are people I can count on in an emergency" (reliable alliance) and "There is someone I could talk to about important decisions in my life" (guidance). Examples of negatively worded items include "Other people do not view me as competent" (reassurance of worth) and "There is no one who relies on me for their well-being" (opportunity for nurturance). This study uses the aggregate scale to measure social support. Responses are scored on a scale of 1 to 5, with 1 representing the lowest and 5 the highest degree of social support. In general, higher levels of social support are expected to reflect a higher-quality work life.

Coaching

The principals in the treatment group were involved in the federally supported research development grant that involved the design and implementation of the structured coaching and mentoring program. The participating school districts hired coaches, typically retired principals, who were trained in the use of a highly structured process that emphasizes the use of coaching as a means of developing instructional leadership skills in new principals.

Coaches met with protégés at least monthly, and each new principal was expected to participate in professional development that focused on specific instructional leadership strategies. The principals implemented this instructional supervision model involving "learning walks" and a structured feedback strategy to work with teachers to improve pedagogy. They also attended monthly cross-district meetings involving several members of the treatment group, designed to provide greater networking and problem-solving opportunities.

Data for the treatment and comparison groups have been denoted using a dummy variable. Participants in the coaching process were scored "1" and members of the comparison group scored "0"; thus, statistical outcomes for this variable in the regression models reflect the net impact of participation in the treatment.

Isolation

The UCLA Loneliness Scale has a long history as a measure of perceptions of isolation for individuals working in a wide variety of settings (Dussault & Thibodeau, 1997; Izgar, 2009; Russell, Cutrona, de la Mora, & Wallace, 1997; Russell, Peplau, & Cutrona, 1980). In this study, a modified version of the most recent scale (Russell, 1996) is used.

This ten-item scale was modified slightly to make it suitable for measuring perceptions of isolation in the work setting. For example, a negatively worded statement from the original scale reads, "I lack companionship" while the same item for this study reads, "I lack companionship at work," while a positive item from the original scale, "I feel left out," was changed to "At work, I feel left out."

Participants responded to items by choosing from the four options of "never," "rarely," "sometimes," or "often," scored on a scale of 1 to 4, with 1 representing the lowest and 4 the highest degree of isolation. Higher scores on this scale reflect greater perceived isolation, which would typically be associated with a more negative assessment of the quality of work life.

Self-Efficacy

Self-efficacy measures principals' beliefs in their abilities to make a difference in the schools they lead. This study employs an instrument developed by Tchannen-Moran and Gareis (2004), an adaptation of a measure introduced by Tschannen-Moran and Woolfolk Hoy (2001). The scale includes 18 items that measure three dimensions of principal efficacy: instructional leadership, management, and moral leadership.

Participants are asked to think about their current role as principal and respond on a nine-point scale regarding the extent to which they can influence a variety of important outcomes at work (1 = not at all, 9 = a great deal). Sample items include "Facilitate student learning in your school?" "Manage change in the school?" and "Promote school spirit among a large majority of the student population?" For purposes of this chapter, the aggregate (total) scale is used, with higher degrees of perceived efficacy reflected in higher scores.

Analytic Procedures

Data for this study were collected using an online survey that permitted participants to access a secure website and complete and submit all answers to the survey directly in electronic form. All principals gave their informed consent before completing and submitting the confidential surveys.

This study focuses on clarifying whether the effect of isolation serves as a mediating factor; that is, whether role stress, social support, and participation in coaching (independent variables) operate through isolation to affect self-efficacy (the dependent variable). As already explained, based on prior literature, it is reasonable to expect higher levels of role stress to be associated with lower levels of efficacy, and higher degrees of social support and participation in coaching to be related to higher levels of efficacy.

While the literature on principal isolation is scant, and evidence relating to new principal isolation virtually nonexistent, there is some evidence that principal isolation contributes to outcomes that reflect the quality of principals' work experience (e.g., Dussault & Thibodeau, 1997).

The following hypotheses summarize a three-step analytic process,[2] and are supported by the literature and conceptual framework. For equation one:

H_1: There will be a statistically significant, positive relationship between the three forms of role stress, and isolation.

H_2: There will be a statistically significant, negative relationship between social support and coaching, and isolation.

For equation two:

H_3: There will be a statistically significant, negative relationship between the three forms of role stress, and self-efficacy.

H_4: There will be a statistically significant, positive relationship between social support and coaching, and self-efficacy.

For equation three:

H_5: Isolation will emerge as a statistically significant, negative predictor of self-efficacy, when controlling for the effects of role stress, social support, and coaching.

To summarize, if these hypotheses are supported, mediation is evident under the condition that the effect of the independent variable on self-efficacy is less in the third equation than in the second.

Statistical significance is reported for each regression model ($p < .05$). To aid in interpretation of findings, we follow Field's (2009) recommendation and computational procedure for determining an effect size statistic associated with each regression statistic to determine practical significance. Field recommends converting the t-statistic to a Pearson correlation (r), "because it's widely understood, [and] frequently used" (p. 332). Thus, in the regression tables, the effect size is reported, labeled "ES." To interpret effect size statistics, we employ Cohen's (1988) suggestion that a small effect is represented by a correlation of .10; a medium effect a correlation of .30; and a large effect a correlation of .50.

Limitations

Several important limitations of this work deserve mention. First, generalizability may be affected by the fact that all participants for this study come from one state in the United States of America. Replicating the study, using a broader national or even international sample of principals, would help support these results as they apply to new principals across the country and the world.

Second, the use of self-reported data in this study leads to criticisms about single-source bias (Podaskoff & Organ, 1987; Spector, 2006). The nature of the variables used for this study cannot be "objectively" measured using another method, however; variables of this nature cannot be "validated" by any reliable external measure. From an epistemological perspective, the use of self-reported data is fitting. Nevertheless, since this study's models are tested using single data sources, statistics may be inflated somewhat; thus, the results should be interpreted with due caution.

RESULTS

This section discusses the study's findings. The following section interprets the meaning of these findings.

Table 5.1 shows the descriptive statistics for all variables in the study, along with Cronbach's alpha for scale measures used in the study as an indicator of reliability. The Cronbach's alpha values range from .74 to .95 and are thus consistent with previous studies, and provide adequate support for the reliability of the data collection instruments utilized.

Descriptive measures need to be examined in the context of the scoring procedures used for each variable. The isolation scale has a score range of 1 to 4; the self-efficacy factor a range of 1 to 9; and all other scales have a score range of 1 to 5. The descriptive statistics, then, show that the study participants report having relatively high levels of social support (mean = 4.34 on a five-point scale), moderate levels of role conflict and overload (means = 2.92 and 3.49, respectively, on a five-point scale), and a slightly lesser degree of perceived role ambiguity (mean = 2.08).

The mean score for the dependent factor, self-efficacy, is 7.15 on a nine-point scale, indicating that on balance, respondents report being efficacious. Respondents report relatively low levels of isolation (mean = 1.75 on a four-point scale), with scores ranging from a low of 1.00 to a high of 3.40. Since coaching is coded as a "dummy" variable, the mean value of .40 on the coaching measure corresponds to the fact that 40% of the new principals in the sample were in the treatment group.

Table 5.1 Descriptive Statistics

	N	Min.	Max.	Mean	SD	Cronbach's Alpha
Ambiguity	197	1.00	4.50	2.08	0.62	.74
Conflict	194	1.14	4.43	2.92	0.70	.83
Overload	196	1.00	5.00	3.49	0.71	.77
Social support	191	3.00	5.00	4.34	0.44	.84
Self-efficacy	196	3.44	9.00	7.15	1.07	.95
Isolation	197	1.00	3.40	1.75	0.57	.90
Coaching	203	0.00	1.00	0.40	0.49	-

Pearson product moment correlations for all of the study variables can be found in Table 5.2. As a result of the relatively large sample size, the majority of the correlation coefficients are statistically significant.[3]

Table 5.3 shows results for the first regression equation, corresponding to stage one in a three-step analytic process, which involves testing the relationships between the independent variables and the mediator, isolation. It was hypothesized that there will be a statistically significant, positive relationship between the three forms of role stress, and isolation; and that there will be a statistically significant, negative relationship between social support and coaching, on the one hand, and isolation.

Results indicate a statistically significant relationship between all of the independent variables together and in isolation, $R^2 = .44$, $F(5, 169) = 26.43$, $p < .01$. The estimates of the regression coefficients show that role ambiguity is a statistically significant predictor of isolation in the expected direction (ß = .19**), i.e., higher levels of role ambiguity are associated with greater isolation.

Social support serves as the most potent predictor of isolation (ß = -.51**), suggesting that greater degrees of social support tend to reduce new principal isolation. This finding is consistent with expectations. Unexpectedly, though, participation in the coaching program emerges as a statistically significant predictor (ß = .14*) in an unexpected fashion, suggesting that principals in the coaching program experience moderately *greater* degrees of isolation. Effect size computations show social support as having a large effect (ES = .53); role ambiguity (ES = .22) and coaching (ES = .17) have small to moderate effects. In contrast to expectations, role overload and role conflict do not emerge as significant predictors of isolation.

The second stage in the analytic process involves regressing self-efficacy on the independent variables. Results for this model are shown in Table 5.4. It was hypothesized that there will be a statistically significant, negative re-

Table 5.2 Zero Order Correlations for Variables in Regression Analysis

	1	2	3	4	5	6	7
1. Ambiguity	--						
2. Conflict	.33	--					
3. Overload	.32	.64	--				
4. Social support	-.23	-.26	-.12	--			
5. Isolation	.34	.32	.19	-.59	--		
6. Coaching	.02	.10	.12	-.12	.21	--	
7. Self-efficacy		-.60	-.34	-.34	.36	-.44	.17	--

Note. All zero-order correlations are statistically significant, $p < .05$, with the exception of those underlined, $p > .05$.

Table 5.3 Regression Analyses: Independent Variables and Isolation (N = 175)

Variable	B (SE)	ß	ES
Dependent variable: isolation			
Role ambiguity	.17 (.06)	.19**	.22
Role conflict	.08 (.06)	.10	.10
Role overload	-.02 (.06)	-.03	.02
Social support	-.66 (.08)	-.51**	.53
Coaching	.16 (.07)	.14*	.17
	$R^2 = .44$ Adj $R^2 = .42$ ($F = 26.43, p < .01$)		

* = $p < .05$; ** = $p < .01$

lationship between role stress and self-efficacy; and that there will be a statistically significant, positive relationship between social support, coaching, and efficacy.

A statistically significant relationship between all of the independent variables and self-efficacy is reported, $R^2 = .47$, $F(5, 166) = 29.23, p < .01$. The estimates of the regression coefficients show that role ambiguity (ß = -.51**) and role overload (ß = -.17*) are statistically significant predictors in the expected direction, implying that lower degrees of ambiguity and overload lead to greater degrees of efficacy. Social support emerges as a statistically significant predictor in the hypothesized direction (ß = .20**), as well. Effect size calculations show that role ambiguity (r = .56) has a large effect, whereas role overload (ES = .17), and social support (ES = .24) each have a small to medium effect on self-efficacy.

Role conflict and participation in the coaching program do not emerge as statistically significant predictors, although participation in the coaching program has a small to medium effect (ES = .15).

Table 5.4 Regression Analyses: Independent Variables and Self-Efficacy (N = 172)

Variable	B (SE)	ß	ES
Dependent variable: self-efficacy			
Role ambiguity	-.89 (.11)	-.51**	.56
Role conflict	.03 (.12)	.02	.02
Role overload	-.26 (.11)	-.17*	.17
Social support	.50 (.15)	.20**	.24
Coaching	-.25 (.13)	-.11	.15
	$R^2 = .47$ Adj $R^2 = .45$ ($F = 29.23, p < .01$)		

* = $p < .05$; ** = $p < .01$

The final step in the analytic process deals with relationships between the independent variables and the mediator, taken together, and the dependent variable. Hypothesis five stated that we expect isolation to emerge as a statistically significant, negative predictor of self-efficacy, even when controlling for the effects of the other independent variables. Mediation will be established if the effects of the role stressors, social support, and coaching on self-efficacy are diminished in these equations as compared with the preceding one. Table 5.5 presents these results.

Results show a statistically significant prediction using all of the independent variables, isolation and self-efficacy, $R^2 = .49$, $F (6, 164) = 26.11$, $p < .01$. The estimates of the regression coefficients show that isolation (ß = -.19*) emerges as a statistically significant predictor of self-efficacy in the expected direction. Social support, however, fails to emerge as a statistically significant predictor (ß = .10), suggesting that isolation serves as a mediator for this variable. Role ambiguity (ß = -.48*) emerges as having a slightly reduced effect on efficacy, although the effect of ambiguity on efficacy remains quite potent and remains statistically significant at the $p < .01$ level.

The impact of role overload (ß = -.17*) is unchanged when accounting for the role of isolation, which suggests that isolation plays no part as a mediator between role overload and self-efficacy. Effect size calculations show that role ambiguity (ES = .50) has a large effect on self-efficacy, whereas role overload (ES = .18) and isolation (ES = .19) each have a small to medium effect. Overall, then, there is support for the assertion that isolation serves as a mediator for social support, but not for any other independent variables in the model.

Table 5.5 Regression Analysis: Independent Variables, Isolation, and Self-Efficacy (N = 171)

Variable	B (SE)	ß	ES
Dependent variable: self-efficacy			
Role ambiguity	-.83 (.11)	-.48**	.50
Role conflict	.05 (.12)	-.04	.04
Role overload	-.26 (.11)	-.17*	.18
Social support	.25 (.18)	.10	.10
Coaching	-.20 (.13)	-.09	.12
Isolation	-.36 (.14)	-.19*	.19
	$R^2 = .49$ Adj $R^2 = .47$ ($F = 26.11$, $p < .01$)		

* = $p < .05$; ** = $p < .01$

DISCUSSION

As a result of the systematic analysis conducted in this study, we present actionable information about the relationship between isolation and self-efficacy for new principals. We have three primary goals for the discussion: (a) given the paucity of empirical work on principal isolation, we seek to add to what is known about the role of isolation in predicting an important work outcome, self-efficacy; (b) by testing the mediation model, we wish to help elaborate existing theory relating to understanding how isolation impacts the work life of principals; and (c) we offer insights into the practice of enhancing new principals' success.

The Relationships among Job Stress, Social Support, and Isolation

Our analysis suggests that the role stress factors of ambiguity and, to a lesser extent, overload, exert an important influence on new principals' sense of efficacy. All else equal, the more intense the degree of role ambiguity and role overload, the lower the level of self-efficacy experienced by new principals. In particular, the strength of the effect of role ambiguity on efficacy is noteworthy. Further, contrary to our initial hypothesis, the relationships between these role stressors and efficacy appear not to be mediated by isolation to any meaningful degree.

An entirely different picture emerges in regard to social support: Whereas social support emerges as a statistically significant predictor of self-efficacy when controlling for role stress and coaching (Table 5.4), this relationship fails to attain significance when accounting for the influence of isolation (Table 5.5). Thus, the impact of social support seems to be fully mediated by the isolation felt by new principals. The lower the levels of social support experienced by new principals, the more isolated they feel, which in turn lessens their sense of self-efficacy.

The connection between social support and isolation is of central interest here. In the abstract, these constructs would seem to be overlapping; indeed, they are highly correlated ($r = -.59$) in the sample used for this study. However, as they are operationalized, social support deals primarily with the mechanisms in place to connect new principals with human resources (e.g., mentoring programs) intended to help them perform better in their jobs. Isolation, in contrast, has to do with the respondent's feelings of connectedness or loneliness. Social support, then, seems to be more structural or procedural in orientation, while isolation has more to do with the individual's emotional state.

The finding that the relationship between social support and self-efficacy is fully mediated by isolation suggests, then, that steps put in place by school systems to promote social support is only likely to impact outcomes such as self-efficacy if the new principal's emotional sense of loneliness or connectedness is impacted. Put another way, social support structures that serve to reduce the degree of isolation felt by new principals would improve their emotional state and enhance self-efficacy.

Coaching or mentoring is one form of social support that is especially prevalent. Among the sample of new principals in this study, however, involvement in a formal coaching program had no statistically significant relationship with reports of self-efficacy when controlling for the influence of the other independent and mediating variables. Coaching may have been seen as having some alternative purpose apart from improving a new principal's prospects for success, but any sort of conclusion about the coaching program would be purely speculative. However, we suggest later in the chapter that coaching that enhances principal involvement in teacher learning appears a promising direction to pursue.

Role ambiguity and role overload appear to be powerful influences on self-efficacy, but they have a modest relationship to new principals' sense of isolation. Both are likely seen as "just part of the job" because of the multiple roles principals play and the ever-shifting nature of expectations for education leaders. Why, then, is reported self-efficacy among new principals so high (mean = 7.15 on a 9-point scale)? One reason for the degree of efficacy reported may be that the new principals in this study experienced relatively low levels of role ambiguity (mean = 2.08) and moderate levels of role overload (mean = 3.49).

Without well-established norms, particularly for principals new to their job, it may be premature to speculate about this. Yet we might speculate that new principals may not have fully confronted the level of role ambiguity and role overload they are likely to face in subsequent years on the job, (nor, we might add, have they been through a full cycle of accountability reporting about their school). In short, they may still be enjoying something of a honeymoon during their first year.

Developing Theory

We demonstrate in this chapter that the effect of social support is fully mediated through isolation; that is, if social support can be enhanced, as interpreted by new principals, isolation is reduced and consequently self-efficacy improves. This suggests that the effect of social support on self-efficacy is best understood as part of a chain reaction. A new model of self-efficacy for new principals acknowledges the role of perceived isolation. It would focus on ways of improving social support to reduce isolation and mitigate the effect of role ambiguity and role overload on self-efficacy.

Furthermore, understanding that social support is mediated by isolation but role ambiguity and role overload are not leads to a reworked model that acknowledges their separate and powerful influence on self-efficacy. This revision of our model appears in Figure 5.2.

A more fully specified theory of self-efficacy for new principals has both research and practical implications. Research-wise, a further elaborated model suggests some logical directions for follow-up studies. On the strength of our theoretical work, quantitative studies should be done to examine the external validity of the model by replicating this work with broader samples of new principals, and work should be done to directly test the implications of the causal model suggested.

Qualitative work to follow up this study can be directed to discover how new principals and central office staff who purport to help them adjust to their challenging job perceive the most effective means to reduce isolation. This kind of research would help to uncover areas of ambiguity and uncertainty that currently cloud our understanding of what principals mean when they report factors such as role stress or the fact that social support efforts actually made them feel somewhat less isolated.

Future model building and research has the potential to inform practice in meaningful ways. It may help central office administrators to think beyond merely inserting structural responses to isolation such as mentoring or coaching programs, focusing them more on what new principals perceive to be helpful and accounting for the growing complexity of the job itself. It also

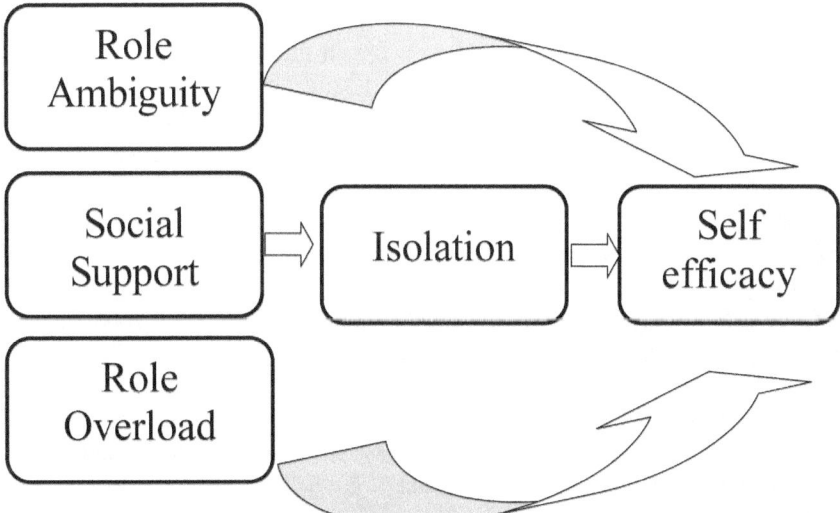

Figure 5.2. Revised Conceptual Framework

has the potential to point the way toward the most important job stress factors so that these can be reduced or eliminated in a manner that enhances self-efficacy.

Improving New Principal Self-Efficacy

New principals may be better supported if school districts communicate with them regularly and openly about their perceptions of role ambiguity and role overload and the degree to which those concerns are being met by whatever support the district provides. This kind of dialogue would, in and of itself, constitute greater social support, but it would also focus other means of social support in ways that are most needed. If the central office can be responsive and mitigate ambiguity and overload, then new principals would likely feel less stressed and less isolated, thus improving their sense of self-efficacy.

The strategy we suggest here is consistent with Donaldson's (2006) conclusions that principals are often overwhelmed by managerial demands and need to be refocused on instruction. In a synthesis of research, Robinson, Lloyd, and Rowe (2008) provide an avenue for doing so. They observe that one of the most potent leadership behaviors that produce significant improvements in student learning is "promoting and participating in teacher learning and development" (p. 663).

In many schools, though, the reality seems to be that professional learning communities are viewed as something principals enable for teachers but do not participate in themselves, and actually participating in teacher learning and development is out of the question given the managerial demands of the job. Thus, freeing new principals to some extent from role ambiguity and role overload would improve their sense of self-efficacy directly and might also allow them to become more involved in teachers' learning—either one-on-one, through established learning communities, or some combination of the two. Participating in teachers' learning would serve to reduce new principals' isolation and, by extension, improve their sense of self-efficacy while attending to the skill-building needs of new leaders.

Stronger networks and more meaningful support from the central office appear likely to reduce new principal isolation and improve self-efficacy. Given the demanding and stressful nature of the principalship, doing so would be no small feat. Knowing that consistent, competent leadership is important to student achievement, reducing new principal isolation, and thus improving their likelihood of success is a critical investment in school and student improvement (Leithwood & Jantzi, 2008).

When self-efficacy declines as a result of increased isolation, instructional improvement is less likely and the probability of new principal success is reduced. The concept of isolation provides a target for promising strategies to help schools and districts maintain more confident and effective leadership.

NOTES

1. Data for this study are a subset of the data compiled for USDE Award #R305E50082, *The Coaching Model: A Collaborative Pilot Program*. The authors would like to gratefully acknowledge the support of the School Leadership Center of Greater New Orleans, the recipient of the grant, and the U.S. Department of Education, Institute for Educational Sciences, National Center for Education Research. The authors take sole responsibility for the work presented.

2. We follow the analytic procedure spelled out by Baron and Kenny (1986) and employ a multistep regression analysis to determine if isolation mediates the relationship between these independent variables and self-efficacy. Using this procedure, mediation is established if the independent variables affect the mediator (equation one); the independent variables affect the dependent variable (equation two); and finally, the mediator affects the dependent variable when controlling for the effects of the independent variables (equation three). Baron and Kenny state: "If these conditions all hold in the predicted direction, then the effect of the independent variable on the dependent variable must be less in the third equation than in the second" (p. 1177).

3. Since the presence of highly correlated independent variables increases the likelihood of multicollinearity in regression analyses, we followed Stevens's (1996) recommendation and examined the Variance Inflation Factors (VIF) to gauge the amount of linear association that occurs between a single component and all of the other factors in the regressions. In general, a VIF that exceeds ten indicates an unacceptable degree of multicollinearity; examination of the VIF for this study shows that none of the VIF values for any independent variable exceed a value of approximately two. On this basis, collinearity does not appear to represent a significant problem.

REFERENCES

Bacharach, S. B., & Aiken, M. (1976). Structural and process constraints on influence in organizations: A level specific analysis. *Administrative Science Quarterly, 21*, 623–642.

Bandura, A. (1977). Self-efficacy: Toward a unifying theory of behavioral change. *Psychological Review, 84*, 191–215.

Bandura, A. (1997). *Self-efficacy: The exercise of control*. New York: W. H. Freeman and Company.

Baron, R. M., & Kenny, D. A. (1986). The moderator-mediator variable distinction in social psychological research: Conceptual, strategic, and statistical considerations. *Journal of Personality and Social Psychology, 51*, 1173–1182.

Bauer, S., Brazer, S., & Stephenson, L. (submitted). The impact of isolation on the job satisfaction of new principals. *Journal of School Leadership*.

Brook, L., Sawyer, E., & Rimm-Kaufman, S. E. (2007). Teacher collaboration in the context of the responsive classroom. *Teachers and Teaching, 13*, 211.

Bunnell, T. (2006). Managing the role stress of public relations practitioners in international schools. *Educational Management Administration & Leadership, 34*, 385–409.

Cohen, J. (1988). *Statistical power analysis for the behavioral sciences*. Mahwah, NJ: Lawrence Erlbaum.

Conley, S., Bacharach, S., & Bauer, S. (1989). The school work environment and teacher career dissatisfaction. *Education Administration Quarterly, 25*, 58–81.

Conley, S., Muncey, D. E., & You, S. (2006) Standards-based evaluation and teacher career satisfaction: A structural equation modeling analysis. *Journal of Personnel Evaluation in Education, 18*, 39–65.

Cookson, P. W. (2005). The challenge of isolation. Professional development—your first year. *Teaching Pre K-8, 36*, 14.

Cuban, L. (1988). *The managerial imperative and the practice of leadership in schools*. Albany: SUNY Press.

Cutrona, C., & Russell, D. (1987). The provisions of social relationships and adaptation to stress. In W. Jones and D. Perlman (Eds.), *Advances in personal relationships, vol. 1* (pp. 37–67). Greenwich, CT: JAI Press.

Cutrona, C., & Russell, D. (1990). Type of social support and specific stress: Toward a theory of optimal matching. In I. G. Sarason, B. R. Sarason, & G. Pierce (Eds.), *Social support: An interactional view* (pp. 319–366). New York: Wiley.

Donaldson, G. (2006). *Cultivating leadership in schools: Connecting people, purpose, and programs* (2nd ed.). New York: Teachers College Press.

Dreeben, R. (1973). The school as a workplace. In R. M. Travers (Ed.), *Second handbook of research on teaching*. Chicago: Rand-McNally.

Dussault, M., & Thibodeau, S. (1997). Professional isolation and performance at work of school principals. *Journal of School Leadership, 7*, 521–536.

Field, A. (2009). *Discovering statistics using SPSS, 3rd ed.* Los Angeles: Sage.

Garmston, R. (2007). Collaborative culture. *Journal of Staff Development, 28*, 55–57.

Gibson, S., & Dembo, M. (1984). Teacher efficacy: A construct validation. *Journal of Educational Psychology, 76*, 569–582.

Glickman, C., Gordon, S., & Ross-Gordon, K. (2004). *Supervision*. Boston: Pearson.

Goddard, R. D., Woolfolk Hoy, A., & Hoy, W. K. (2004). Collective efficacy beliefs: Theoretical developments, empirical evidence, and future directions. *Educational Researcher, 33*(3), 3–13.

Guskey, T. R., & Passaro, P. (1994). Teacher efficacy: A study of construct dimensions. *American Educational Research Journal, 31*, 627–643.

Herrington, A., Herrington, J., Kervin, L., & Ferry, B. (2006). The design of an online community of practice for beginning teachers. *Contemporary Issues in Technology and Teacher Education, 6*, 120–132.

Hobson, A. J., & Sharp, C. (2005). Head to head: A systematic review of the research evidence on mentoring new head teachers. *School Leadership and Management, 25*, 25–42.

Hord, S. M. (2007). Learn in community with others. *Journal of Staff Development, 28*, 39–42.
Howard, M. P., & Mallory, B. J. (2008). Perceptions of isolation among high school principals. *Journal of Women in Education Leadership, 6*, 7–27.
Hoy, W. K., Sweetland, S. R., & Smith, P. A. (2002). Toward an organizational model of achievement in high schools: The significance of collective efficacy. *Educational Administration Quarterly, 38*, 77–93.
Izgar, H. (2009). An investigation of depression and loneliness among school principals. *Educational Sciences: Theory & Practice, 9*, 247–258.
Leithwood, K., & Jantzi, D. (2008). Linking leadership to student learning: The contributions of leader efficacy. *Educational Administration Quarterly, 44*, 496–528.
Leithwood, K., Louis, K. S., Anderson, S., & Wahlstrom, K. (2004). *How leadership influences student learning*. New York: The Wallace Foundation.
Marshall, G. W., Michaels, C. E., & Mulki, J. P. (2007). Workplace isolation: Exploring the construct and its measurement. *Psychology and Marketing, 24*, 195–223.
Norton, J. (2001). Sharing the mystery. *Journal of Staff Development, 22*, 51–54.
Norton, M. (2003). Let's keep our quality school principals on the job. *High School Journal, 86*, 50–56.
Podaskoff, P. M., & Organ, D. W. (1987). Self reports in organizational research: Problems and prospects. *Journal of Management, 12*, 531–544.
Rizzo, J. R., House, R. J., & Lirtzman, S. I. (1970). Role conflict and ambiguity in complex organizations. *Administrative Science Quarterly, 15*, 150–163.
Robbins, P., & Alvey, H. B. (2003). *The principal's companion: Strategies and hints to make the job easier*. Thousand Oaks, CA: Corwin Press.
Robinson, V. M., Lloyd, C. A., & Rowe, K. J. (2008). The impact of leadership on student outcomes: An analysis of the differential effects of leadership styles. *Educational Administration Quarterly, 44*, 635–674.
Russell, D. (1996). The UCLA Loneliness Scale (Version 3): Reliability, validity, and factor structure. *Journal of Personality Assessment, 66*, 20–24.
Russell, D., Cutrona, C. E., de la Mora, A., & Wallace, R. B. (1997). Loneliness and nursing home admission among the rural elderly. *Psychology and Aging, 12*, 574–589.
Russell, D., Peplau, L. A., & Cutrona, C. E. (1980). The revised UCLA Loneliness Scale: Concurrent and discriminant validity evidence. *Journal of Personality and Social Psychology, 39*, 472–548.
Schlechte, J., Yssel, N., & Merbler, J. (2005). Case studies in teacher isolation and alienation. *Preventing School Failure, 50*, 35.
Spector, P. E. (2006). Method variance as an artifact in self-report affect and perceptions at work: Myth or significant problem? *Journal of Applied Psychology, 72*, 438–44.
Stephenson, L., & Bauer, S. (forthcoming). The role of isolation in predicting new principals' burnout. *International Journal of Educational Policy and Leadership*.
Stevens, J. (1996). *Applied multivariate statistics for the social sciences* (3rd ed.). Mahwah, NJ: Lawrence.
Tschannen-Moran, M., & Gareis, C. R. (2004). Principals' sense of efficacy: Assessing a promising construct. *Journal of Educational Administration, 42*, 573–585.

Tschannen-Moran, M., & Woolfolk Hoy, A. (2001). Teacher efficacy: Capturing an elusive construct. *Teaching and Teacher Education, 17*, 783–805.

Waters, T., Marzano, R., & McNulty, B. (2003). *Balanced leadership: What 30 years of research tells us about the effect of leadership on student achievement.* Denver, CO: Mid-Continent Research for Education and Learning.

Weiss, R. S. (1974). The provisions of social relationships. In Z. Rubin (Ed.), *Doing unto Others* (pp. 17–26). Englewood Cliffs, NJ: Prentice-Hall.

Wong, S., DeSanctis, G., & Staudenmayer, N. (2007). The relationship between task interdependency and role stress: A revisit of the job demands-control model. *Journal of Management Studies, 44*, 284–303.

Appendix 5.1. Sample Items for Survey Measures

Variable	# items	Sample Items
Role ambiguity	4	For each statement, please indicate the response that best describes your current job: (1 = strongly disagree, 5 = strongly agree) - I feel certain about how much authority I have* - I know exactly what is expected of me*
Role conflict	7	For each statement, please indicate the response that best describes your current job: (1 = strongly disagree, 5 = strongly agree) - I work with two or more groups who operate quite differently - I receive incompatible requests from two or more people
Role overload	6	For each statement, please indicate the response that best describes your current job: (1 = strongly disagree, 5 = strongly agree) - I cannot ever seem to catch up - I have to do things I do not really have the time and energy for
Social support	16	Read each of the following items and decide which choice best indicates how you feel about relationships with others at work (1 = strongly disagree, 5 = strongly agree) - There are people I can count on in an emergency - There are people who depend on me for help - There is no one I can turn to for guidance in times of stress*
Isolation	10	The following statements describe how people sometimes feel about their work. For each statement, please indicate how often you feel the way described by selecting the best answer in the space provided. (1 = never, 4 = always) - I lack companionship at work - At work, I feel left out - I feel isolated from others at work
Self-efficacy	18	In your current role as principal, to what extent can you . . . (1 = not at all, 9 = a great deal) - Facilitate student learning in your school? - Manage change in the school? - Promote school spirit among a large majority of the student population?

* agreement with this item indicates a low value of the variable

Chapter Six

Assistant Superintendents Moving to the Superintendency

David F. Leach and Bruce S. Cooper

Although research on district-level leadership is extensive for the superintendent of schools, for reasons unclear, the *assistant* (or deputy/associate) *superintendent* has been virtually ignored. This omission is troublesome because the assistant's post is usually the stepping-stone to the top job. Since superintendents are in short supply and often enter their first superintendency late in their careers —a mass exodus is imminent—we need to understand and nurture the assistants to prepare them to step into the critical leadership role (Sutton, Jobe, McCord, Jordan, & Jordan, 2008; Glass & Franceschini, 2007).

We know that most school superintendents have previously served in one or more of the following key leadership roles: district office administrator (e.g., deputy superintendent, assistant superintendent, director, coordinator), elementary principal, middle school principal, and/or a high school principal, and teacher. Dana and Bourisaw (2006) map out the common career paths as follows:

> The candidates for superintendents are most often those who follow a common career path. That path involves five to six years of teaching, assistant principal, principal, assistant superintendent, and superintendent. Leadership positions (director, coordinator, etc.) may exist between the school principal position and assistant superintendent position, particularly in a large school district. And, of course, the career path can be abbreviated—principal, assistant superintendent, superintendent—and sometimes can be an alternative path. Commonly, though, the path is a five-step process. (p. 34)

Thus, the field of educational leadership today faces the problem that while the majority of superintendents throughout the nation plan to retire in the next few years, we know very little about their logical successors—assistant, associate, and deputy superintendents. Researchers aver that strong school district leadership positively affects student achievement and warn that the size and quality of the superintendent applicant pools are continuing to diminish. If this state of affairs goes unheeded, concerns over the quality and quantity of future school superintendents remain salient and complex.

As leaders in their own right, assistant superintendents also occupy a strategic position in the day-to-day operation of school districts and schools too. For example, they can help prepare and support school principals (Butler, 2008). Equally important, they often serve as important advisors and confidants to the superintendents (Cooper & Fusarelli, 2004). In fact, the success and longevity of school superintendents may hinge on the contributions of their assistant superintendent(s) (Whritner, 2009), who often work as part of a cadre of prospective candidates who have had the opportunity to gain relevant experience.

Many assistant superintendents witness firsthand how the demands of the superintendency can adversely affect a person's quality of life. For instance, they see superintendents' contracts, salaries, and family lives being closely watched by many of their constituents, with this exposure to public scrutiny and a loss of any private life discouraging some from pursuing the position. Cetorelli (1997) found that qualified candidates who elected not to seek the superintendency expressed that a major discouragement was their "concern about the poorer quality of life for a superintendent, including loss of privacy" (p. 281).

Assistant superintendents also witness the combative relationships that can exist between a superintendent and the board of education. Superintendents often assign their assistant superintendents prominent roles when interacting with their board of education (Petersen & Fusarelli, 2001), where they gain firsthand experience with interacting with the board of education. Yet such interactions do not always have positive consequences. As Dlott (2007) reports, based on his own experience,

> As an assistant superintendent, I learned about the dangers of school board/superintendent conflict by witnessing a modern-day defenestration of my one-time boss. The only thing lacking in this defenestration was an actual window and the ceremonial throw. All the other elements of the humiliation and pain of being stripped of power were present. (p. 101)

Such experiences can deter qualified candidates from pursuing the superintendency. In a study of the qualified candidates in Colorado who elected not to pursue the superintendency, Hodges (2005) found that board relations was a deterrent for many prospective candidates. Specifically, dealing with board members' personal agendas (43.6%) and facing potential power struggles with the board (31.62%) convinced many assistant superintendents to go no further.

In sum, superintendents and assistant superintendents' attention is often distracted from a concern about the well-being of their students, to the more mundane or politically charged tasks. Unfortunately, these assistant superintendents make up the shrinking pool of qualified superintendent candidates.

Throughout the country, an examination of advertisements for the position of school superintendent in the classified sections of local papers indicates that school boards usually seek superintendent candidates with central office experience, as well as administrators who have held districtwide responsibilities and who think systemically.

While many school building administrators may have the training and certification necessary to become a superintendent—along with some relevant administrative experience—their expertise is typically only as broad as their building-level leadership rather than being districtwide. It seems timely, therefore, to gauge how interested today's assistant superintendents are in pursing the superintendency, given that they are next in line and often best prepared for the rigors of the job.

STATEMENT OF THE PROBLEM

The purpose of this quantitative study is to examine the assistant school superintendent: specifically, to determine the characteristics of the educators who fulfill these roles in our schools, their job responsibilities inherent to their position as school assistant superintendent, and their sense of job satisfaction/dissatisfaction and job efficacy. Furthermore, the study seeks to determine the assistant, associate, and deputy superintendents' aspirations to become a superintendent in their future—to stay put or "move up" the proverbial career ladder to the top (the "precipice") in the school district.

Research Questions

The following four research questions guided this study:

1. What key demographic characteristics (e.g., gender, ethnicity, age, experience, background degrees, etc.) best describe the typical incumbent assistant, deputy, and associate superintendents, employed in one state's public school systems?
2. What job roles and responsibilities are common to incumbent assistant, deputy, and associate superintendents employed in local public school districts?
3. To what degree do incumbent assistant, deputy, and associate school superintendents (a) express a sense of satisfaction or dissatisfaction with their

jobs, (b) perceive a sense of job efficacy, and (c) express their intention to pursue the superintendency in their future career?

4. How do job roles, working conditions, board of education relationships, and interactions with the community and the superintendent of incumbent New York State assistant, deputy, and associate school superintendents relate to their (a) sense of job satisfaction, (b) perceptions of job efficacy, and (c) desire to become superintendents?

To date, most studies, including the *2007 State of the Superintendency Mini-Survey: Aspiring to the Superintendency*, sought the opinions of incumbent superintendents—not *prospective* candidates, such as assistant superintendents. The time has come to learn more about the career of the assistant superintendent and to shed light on the causes of this shrinking pool of superintendent candidates and offer ideas and recommendations that will attract more members of this talented group to pursue the top leadership post in education.

RESEARCH DESIGN

The design of the study, presented in Figure 6.1, explores the relationship between the independent variables (personal demographics, professional profile, and school district demographics) with the intervening variables (interaction with community, working conditions, interaction with superintendents, relationship with boards of education, and job roles) to determine the assistant, associate, and deputy school superintendents' sense of job efficacy, job satisfaction, and career aspirations.

Instrumentation

The researchers developed a 50-item questionnaire specifically for use in this study called the *Assistant Superintendents' Professional Incentives, Roles, and Efficacy* or *ASPIRE*. The instrument was examined using ten variables as follows:

1. Personal demographic and professional profile
2. School district profile
3. Interaction with the community
4. Interaction with the superintendent
5. Working conditions
6. Role involvement
7. Board of education relations

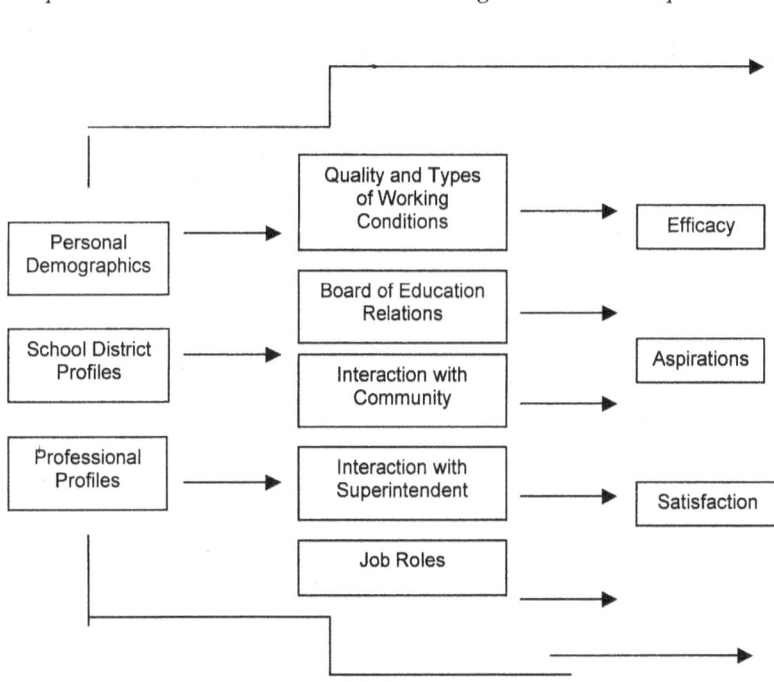

Figure 6.1. Research Study Design of Assistant Superintendents of Schools

8. Career aspirations
9. Job satisfaction
10. Job efficacy

In all sections, except for "role involvement," the study used a 5-point Likert scale (1 = *strongly disagree* to 5 = *strongly agree*) with select items. For "role involvement," a 4-point scale was used instead (1 = *none* to 4 = *high*) to indicate role involvement. The instrument was tested for validity and reliability before being used in the present research. To ensure content validity, using the Latham-Wexley method (Latham, Wexley, & Pursell, 1975), the survey items were reviewed by a group of 30 doctoral students who were familiar with the important role variables of the various types of assistant superintendents.

Participants received a copy of the survey items, listed in a random manner, and categorized the items under one of the aforementioned 10 variable categories. An item was removed if fewer than 80% of the participants agreed on its placement. Cronbach's alpha was used to measure internal consistency for each construct. All subscales achieved a reliability coefficient of at least .70 or above to ensure the ASPIRE's internal consistency.

Sample and Data Collection

An electronic survey (see Dillman, 2007; Gall, Gall, & Borg, 2007; Yun & Trumbo, 2000) on the website Zoomerang.com provided secure Internet access to gather data. The researchers used this website to post the *ASPIRE* questionnaire online, collect the responses, and review the results.

The roster of possible respondents was obtained from two sources: First, the researchers approached the New York State Education Department (NYSED), which provided a current list of all assistant, associate, and deputy superintendents. The NYSED sorted their 2007–2008 Basic Education Data System to create an electronic spreadsheet that included approximately 230 assistant, associate, and deputy superintendents statewide and provided the following information: district name, participants' last name, first name, assignment description, years in district, degree, salary, and district address.

Next, the researchers surveyed individual school district websites and administrative directories to locate assistant superintendents for the NYSED list, adding 100 more participants to the sample. E-mail addresses for possible participants were obtained by perusing school districts' websites or by contacting the Boards of Cooperative Educational Services (BOCES) located in the assistant superintendents' respective regions. The spreadsheet was revised and updated to reflect the 2008–2009 school year, allowing the researchers to compile a list of all known New York State assistant, associate, or deputy superintendents and their verified e-mail addresses.

The first step in data collection was to e-mail an invitation to participate in the survey, via the Zoomerang.com website, including the 330 assistant, associate, and deputy superintendents who represented all known professionals in these roles in New York State. The invitation contained a link to the online survey, meaning that the researchers had no contact with the participants other than through the e-mail invitation. Participants were informed about the research, its purposes, and how data would be collected and analyzed.

Therefore, the online survey software was programmed to ensure that neither the researchers nor anyone involved with this survey could capture those data. Any reports or publications based on this research used only group data and did not identify any participant as being affiliated with this project.

Limitations

This study is limited to a sample of assistant, associate, and deputy school superintendents employed only in New York State. Because of a recent reorganization of the New York City Department of Education, assistant superintendents from New York City public schools were excluded from the study. Furthermore, the data in this study are restricted to self-report survey data, with no interviews or observational data on the work of assistant superintendents.

Likewise, it was beyond the scope of this study to collect information on the participants' colleagues or supervisors' perceptions about how well the respondents were doing in their job. Despite these limitations, the findings of this study are helpful to those interested in learning more about the assistant, associate, and deputy superintendents, while providing some leads on how to solve the problem of the shortage of qualified candidates for superintendent positions in public schools and to gain insight into the role of assistant superintendents and their crucial career decisions.

FINDINGS

Demographic Profiles

A review of the literature prior to conducting this study was unable to locate documented research on the personal and professional characteristics of assistant superintendents in New York State. Thus, the results of this study provide a rare glimpse into their typical demographic data. Table 6.1 presents data related to the 159 respondents' age, gender, ethnicity, and district location.

We solicited an equal number of male (49.7%) and female (50.3%) respondents, with about half (50.3%) reporting being between 50 and 59 years of age; nearly one-third (32.7%) indicated being between 40 and 49 years old, and none were under 30 years of age.

Table 6.1 Demographic Profile of Survey Assistant Superintendent Respondents (N = 159)

Demographics	N	Percent
Gender		
Male	79	49.7
Female	80	50.3
Total	159	100.0
Age		
30–39	10	6.3
40–49	52	32.7
50–59	80	50.3
60 or older	17	10.7
Total	159	100.0

Promoted to Current Position Internally/Externally

Respondents were then asked if they had occupied a prior position in their *current* district as an indication of the extent of internal promotions (see Carlson, 1962, 1972). For purposes of clarity and brevity, the four types of assistant superintendent respondents in the study are, from this point on, referred to in terms of their self-reported roles/functions, as follows: *Generalist* = assistant or deputy or associate, *Curriculum* = curriculum specialist, *Personnel* = personnel specialist, and *Business* = business specialist. As shown in Table 6.2, districts appear to be more likely to hire internal candidates (current district employees) to the positions of curriculum (59.7%), and personnel (36.4%) assistant superintendents compared to business assistant superintendents (10%).

Overall, we see that over half (55%) of the sample assistant superintendents had been hired for their current post from *outside the school district*, showing the mobility of the position, as candidates move into the number-two post in the central office.

Salary Range in Current Position (see Table 6.3)

The respondents reported that current salary (excluding benefits and annuities) ranged from below $100,000 to over $200,000. Just over half (52.8%) of the respondents reported salaries in the $140,000–$199,999 range, with only a small minority (8.9%) reporting salaries higher than $200,000 (median salary range = $150,000–$159,999). All respondents who reported earning over $200,000 also reported working in the wealthier Downstate Suburban Region of the state.

Job Satisfaction

The New York State assistant school superintendent respondents in this study indicated high levels of job satisfaction, with a mean of 4.33 out of 5.0 and a

Table 6.2 Internal versus External Promotion Data by Job Specialty (N = 153)

Current Assistant Superintendent Position	Occupied Prior Position in *Current* District					
	Yes		No		Total	
	n	%	n	%	N	%
Generalist	18	45.0	22	55.0	40	100.0
Business	3	10.0	27	90.0	30	100.0
Curriculum	43	59.7	29	40.3	72	100.0
Personnel	4	36.4	7	63.6	11	100.0
Total	68	44.0	85	55.0	153	100.0

Table 6.3 Salary Range in Current Position (Excluding Benefits/Annuities) (N = 157)

Salary Range	N	%
Below $100,000	1	0.6
$100,000–$119,999	32	20.4
$120,000–$139,999	27	17.2
$140,000–$159,999	30	19.1
$160,000–$179,999	28	17.8
$180,000–$199,999	25	15.9
Over $200,000	14	8.9
Total	157	100.0

standard deviation of .76 (see Table 6.4) and had almost as high a level of satisfaction with their pay and fringe benefits (mean = 3.99; range 1–5). Put another way, approximately 93% of the respondents indicated that they "agreed" (4.0) or "strongly agreed" (5.0) that their work gave them real job satisfaction.

Job Efficacy

The assistant school superintendent respondents also indicated high levels of a sense of being effective in their role, showing a mean of 4.43 with a SD of .55 (see Table 6.4) and providing effective leadership in their districts (mean = 4.42; SD = .58). Again, put another way, 97% of the respondents reported a "very high level of job efficacy" in their role as an assistant superintendent.

Career Aspirations

Several items in the *ASPIRE* survey explored the assistant superintendents' career aspirations for their future work in education.

Desire to Become a Superintendent

Their responses to "I see myself assuming the role of superintendent of schools" are illustrated below in Figure 6.2. Although only about one-quarter (27%) of the respondents indicate that they aspire to become a superintendent, importantly 31% remain undecided. Thus, almost three-fourths (73%) report that they are either undecided or will not pursue a superintendency.

Disincentives to Becoming a Superintendent

Their responses to statements that were specific disincentives associated with pursing the superintendency—for example, family sacrifices; the low

Table 6.4 Mean Score for Key Variables for the Total Sample of Assistant Superintendents (N = 159)

Variables	Mean	SD
INTERVENING VARIABLES		
1. Interaction with community	3.70	0.94
2. Interaction with the superintendent	4.48	0.78
3. Working conditions	4.20	0.92
4. Board of education relations	4.44	0.71
DEPENDENT VARIABLES		
CAREER ASPIRATIONS		
1. Desire to become a superintendent (scale 1–3)	2.04	0.78
2. Preference to be promoted to superintendency in current district	3.37	1.15
3. Willingness to relocate to move into a superintendency	2.78	1.35
4. Distance they are willing to commute to work	2.79	1.24
5. Anticipated time frame to obtain a superintendency	2.60	1.30
6. Disincentives associated with pursuing a superintendency		
a. Family sacrifices are important reasons why I do not pursue a superintendency.	3.28	1.22
b. The salary level is low in comparison to the level of responsibility is an important reason why I do not pursue a superintendency.	2.74	1.07
c. The lack of funding for public schools is an important reason why I do not pursue a superintendency.	2.57	0.99
d. Local politics is an important reason why I do not pursue a superintendency	3.27	1.18
JOB SATISFACTION		
1. My work as an assistant superintendent has given me real job satisfaction.	4.33	0.76
2. I am satisfied with the amount of pay and fringe benefits I receive.	3.99	0.93
JOB EFFICACY		
1. Overall, I am effective in my role as assistant superintendent.	4.43	0.55
2. I effectively provide leadership throughout my district.	4.42	0.58

salaries given the levels of responsibility; local politics; and the lack of funding for public schools—are presented in Figure 6.3. The strongest disincentives indicated by the assistant superintendent respondents were family sacrifices (with 63% agreed or strongly agreed) and local politics (59% agreed or strongly agreed). In contrast, a lack of public funding (22% agreed or strongly agreed) or the low salaries given the high level of responsibilities (33% agreed or strongly agreed) were seen as disincentives by a much smaller percentage.

Assistant Superintendents Moving to the Superintendency 123

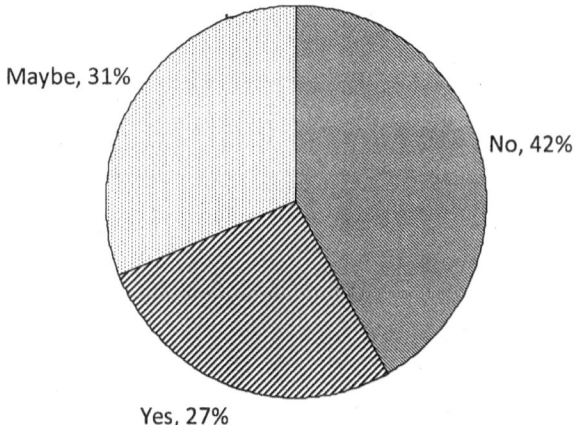

Figure 6.2. Intent to Pursue the Superintendency by All Respondents (*n* = 159)

Preferences Related to Becoming a Superintendent

Respondents who indicated that they will or may obtain a superintendency (*n* = 92) were asked for four more points about their willingness and preferences related to becoming a superintendent.

In response to "When would you like to attain a superintendency?" almost one-third of the respondents (30%) indicated that they would like this to occur immediately, with another one-third (27%) showing that

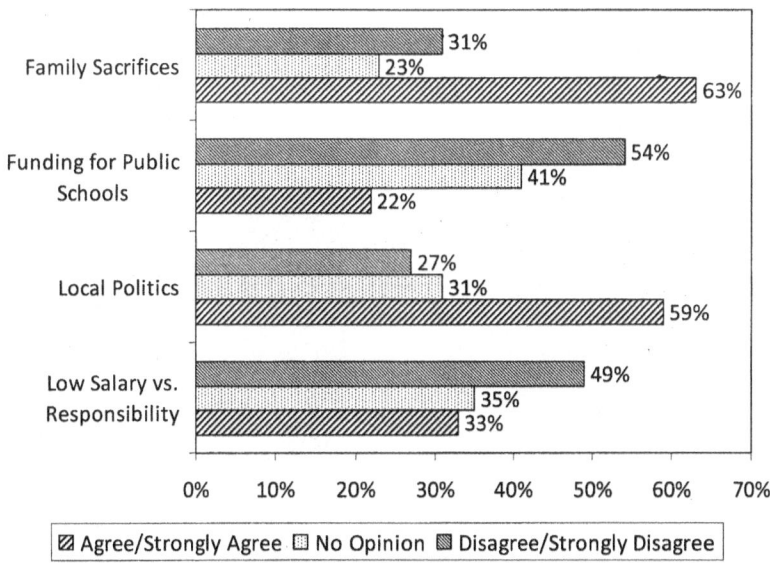

Figure 6.3. Disincentives for Becoming a Superintendent (*n* = 117)

they would like to become a superintendent within about 3 to 5 years (see Figure 6.4).

In response to "I prefer to be promoted to superintendent within my current school district," surprisingly, about half of the respondents (49%) indicated that they have no preference in this area, and another 15% indicated they would prefer *not* to remain in their current district. This finding shows that about 65% are not "place-bound" to their current district, to use Carlson's terminology (1962).

A set of items sought to gauge how eager they were to pursue a superintendency. One-third of them reported being willing to relocate (33%) and almost an equal number indicated a willingness to commute over 40 miles if it meant obtaining a superintendent position.

Key Intervening Variables

Overall, the vast majority of the assistant superintendent respondents agreed or strongly agreed that their *relationships* with their community (85%), superintendent (95%), and board of education (92%) are positive (see Figure 6.5). The means for these four variables ranged from 4.48 to 3.70 on a 5-point scale, where the higher the score, the more positive the response (see Table 6.4). An equally large percentage (94%, see Figure 6.5) agreed or

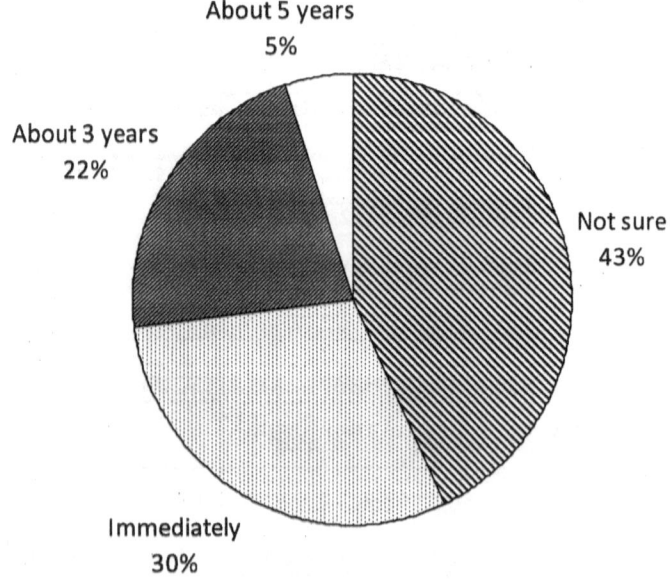

Figure 6.4. Time Frame for Becoming a Superintendent (*n* = 92)

strongly agreed that their work conditions are favorable (mean = 4.20; range 1–5, see Table 6.4).

Interestingly, the study also found that while 85% of the respondents "agreed" or "strongly agreed" with the statement "Strong support exists in my community for education," only 48% agreed or strongly agreed with "The community has a good understanding of my role." Similarly, while 94% of respondents agreed or strongly agreed that "Overall, my work conditions are favorable," a smaller percentage (75%) agreed or strongly agreed with the statement "I have sufficient support personnel/staff."

Moreover, while 95% of respondents agreed or strongly agreed with the statement "I have a good relationship with my superintendent," a smaller number (84%) view their superintendent to be a "positive mentor" for them.

Comparison by Group Characteristics

This section presents the results of an analysis of the survey data using t-tests and an ANOVA to explore whether superintendents' attitudes and behaviors are significantly different when grouped and compared by age, gender, and role.

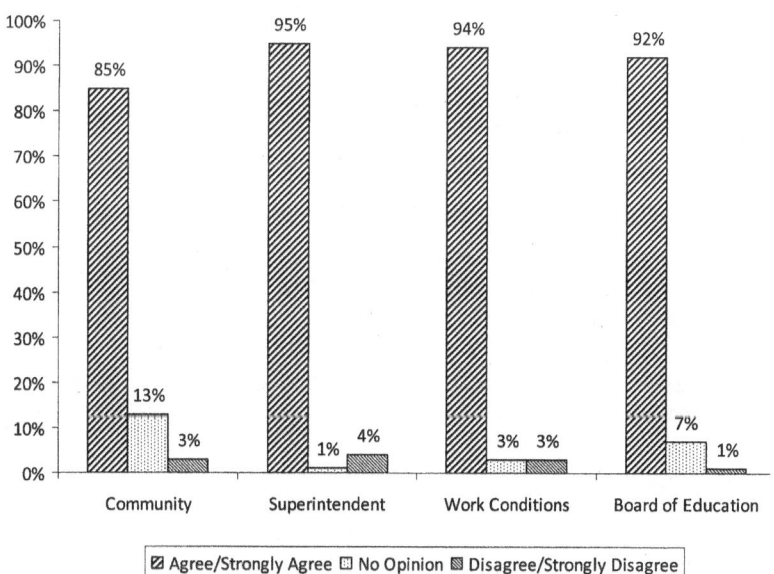

Figure 6.5. Assistant Superintendents' Perceptions of Their Relationships with the Superintendent, Community, and Board of Education, and of Their Work Conditions (n = 159)

Age

Null hypothesis 1: There will be no significant difference between assistant superintendents at ages 39 to 49 and ages 50 or older, and their level of job satisfaction, job efficacy, and aspirations to become a superintendent. The data of the two age cohorts are shown in Table 6.5.

In particular, the assistant superintendents' overall *job satisfaction* scores were significantly different as a function of age, with those 50 years of age or older having significantly higher mean job satisfaction scores than those 49 years of age or younger (means = 4.44 compared to 4.16, respectively, $p = .025$).

Similarly, the assistant superintendents' overall *job efficacy* scores were significantly different as a function of age, with those 50 years of age or older having a higher mean job efficacy score than those 49 years of age or younger (4.51 vs. 4.31, respectively, which was significant at the $p = .024$ level) (see Table 6.5).

The assistant superintendents' overall *career aspiration*, or desire to pursue a superintendency, scores were also significantly different as a *function of age*, with those 50 years of age or older having a highly significant lower mean score than those 49 years of age or younger (1.96 compared to 2.49, respectively, $p = .001$) (see Table 6.5).

Gender

Next we tested the Null Hypothesis 3: There will be no significant difference between male and female assistant superintendents in their levels of job satisfaction, job efficacy, aspirations to become a superintendent, and their perceptions of the community as possessing a good understanding of their role.

As the data in Table 6.6 indicate, the sample assistant superintendents' overall job satisfaction scores and aspiration to become a superintendent were significantly different as a function of gender.

Female respondents had a higher mean job *satisfaction* score than did their male peers (4.46 vs. 4.19, $p = .026$) (see Table 6.6). On the other hand,

Table 6.5 Results of T-Tests: Job Satisfaction, Job Efficacy, and Career Aspirations by Assistant Superintendents' Age (N = 159)

Variables	49 years or younger ($n = 62$)		50 years or older ($n = 97$)		F	P
	Mean	SD	Mean	SD		
Job satisfaction	4.16	0.79	4.44	0.72	1.10	.03
Job efficacy	4.31	0.56	4.51	0.52	0.36	.02
Career aspirations	2.49	0.88	1.96	1.00	29.43	.00

Table 6.6. Results of T-Tests: Job Satisfaction, Job Efficacy, Career Aspirations, and Perceptions of Community Support by Assistant Superintendents' Gender (N = 159)

Variables	Female (n = 80) Mean	SD	Male (n = 70) Mean	SD	F	P
Dependent Variables						
Job satisfaction	4.46	0.67	4.19	0.82	0.04	.03
Job efficacy	4.49	0.50	4.37	0.58	1.49	.18
Career Aspirations as Aspirations	2.00	1.01	2.34	0.95	10.45	.03
Intervening Variables						
Community support	4.01	0.83	4.25	0.63	0.03	.05

males had higher *job aspiration* scores, on wanting to become a superintendent, than did the females (2.34 compared to 2.00, $p = .029$) although both means were low. But no differences in their sense of *job efficacy* were found as a function of gender. However, significant differences were found in assistant superintendents' perception of the community possessing a good understanding of their role as a function of their gender, with males having more positive perceptions of their community than did the females (4.25 vs. 4.01, $p = .049$).

Differences by Role Functions

Next, the research tested Null Hypothesis 5: No significant difference will emerge among the assistant superintendents' role function (generalist, curriculum, business versus personnel) and their level of job satisfaction, sense of job efficacy, and aspirations to become a superintendent.

As the data in Tables 6.7 and 6.8 indicate, with regard to *job satisfaction*, the Generalists had the highest mean score (4.54) compared with Curriculum

Table 6.7 Means and Standard Deviations, Assistant Superintendents' Job Roles by Job Satisfaction, Job Efficacy, and Career Aspirations (N = 159)

	Assistant Superintendents' Job Roles							
	Generalist (n = 40)		Curriculum (n = 75)		Business (n = 32)		Personnel (n = 11)	
Variables	Mean	SD	Mean	SD	Mean	SD	Mean	SD
Job satisfaction	4.54	0.56	4.31	0.82	4.31	0.47	3.73	1.27
Job efficacy	4.58	0.50	4.35	0.56	4.41	0.56	4.45	0.52
Career aspirations	2.45	0.90	2.33	0.95	1.56	0.91	1.73	1.00

Table 6.8 Results of an ANOVA of Comparisons between and within Groups for Assistant Superintendents' Job Roles by Job Satisfaction, Job Efficacy, and Career Aspirations (N = 159)

		Sum of Squares	Df	Mean Square	F	p
Job satisfaction	Between groups	5.74	3	1.91	3.46	.02
	Within groups	84.70	153	0.55		
	Total	90.43	156			
Job efficacy	Between groups	1.32	3	0.44	1.50	.22
	Within groups	45.09	153	0.30		
	Total	46.41	156			
Aspiration to become a superintendent	Between groups	19.10	3	6.37	7.28	.00
	Within groups	134.62	154	0.87		
	Total	153.72	157			

(4.31), Business (4.31), and Personnel (3.73) functions ($p = .02$). It appears that the *Generalists*, those holding broader responsibilities (i.e., deputy and assistant superintendent titles), viewed their role to be more satisfying than their colleagues who served in more specialized function (i.e., assistant superintendent of business, personnel, or curriculum).

Similarly, regarding the aspiration to become a superintendent, the Generalists reported the highest mean score (2.45), compared with Curriculum (2.33), Business (1.56), and Personnel (1.73) functions ($pQ10 = .000$). Finally, for job efficacy, the differences in the four groups' mean scores were insignificant among the four functional-occupational groups.

Correlation Analyses

Pearson product-moment correlations were computed to determine the level of relationships between various independent, intervening, and dependent variables in this study. This correlation analysis sought to test the following null hypotheses.

Hypothesis 6: There will be no significant relationship between the assistant superintendents' sense of work conditions, relationships with their board of education, community, and superintendent, and their level of job satisfaction and sense of job efficacy.

Hypothesis 7: There will be no significant correlation between the assistant superintendents' age and specific role involvement and their aspirations to become a superintendent.

Hypothesis 8: There will be no significant correlation between the assistant superintendents' willingness to relocate, travel/commute a distance of 40 miles to work, and time frame to obtain a superintendency and their aspirations to become a superintendent.

The first correlation addressed Hypothesis 6, as shown in Table 6.9. Job satisfaction had a moderate, positive, and significant ($p = .01$) correlation with job efficacy ($r = .47$), leadership fulfillment ($r = .45$), and work conditions ($r = .49$), and a slightly lower one with salary contentment ($r = .35$). Job satisfaction also had a significant ($p = .01$) and positive but low relationship with community awareness of their role ($r = .22$), relationship with superintendent ($r = .27$), and board of education role support ($r = .27$). It had a significant, but negative and low, correlation with school district socioeconomic status ($r = -.26, p = .01$).

The assistant superintendents' sense of job efficacy had a very positive, high, and significant relation with leadership fulfillment ($r = .81, p = .01$). It had a significant ($p = .01$) and positive, but low ($r = .20$ to $r = .30$) correlation with salary contentment, community awareness of their roles, relationship with superintendent, board of education support, and work conditions. Thus, the null hypothesis was rejected.

Additional correlation analyses addressed Hypotheses 6, 7, and 8, which focused on the relationship between the assistant superintendents' *aspirations* to become a superintendent and other select variables. The data in Table 6.9

Table 6.9 Correlations between Selected Intervening and Independent Variables and Sample Superintendents' Job Satisfaction and Job Efficacy (N = 159)

Variables				Variables					
	1	2	3	4	5	6	7	8	9
1 Job satisfaction	—								
2 Job efficacy	.47**	—							
3 Age	.16*	.14	—						
4 District socio-economic status	-.26*	-.03	.02	—					
5 Salary contentment	.35**	.20*	.14	-.26**	—				
6 Leadership fulfillment	.45**	.81**	.19*	-.03	.22**	—			
7 Community awareness	.22**	.23**	.03	-.20*	.36**	.28**	—		
8 Relationship with superintendent	.27**	.21**	-.07	.05	.10	.21**	.17*	—	
9 Board of education support	.27**	.23**	.04	-.05	.36**	.24**	.42**	.23*	—
10 Work conditions	.49**	.30**	.08	-.13	.44**	.31**	.38**	.38**	.41**

* Correlation at .05 level (2-tailed). ** Correlation at .01 level (2-tailed).

show an inverse and low relationship between assistant superintendents' career aspirations to become a superintendent and their age, educational level, and recruitment to become a superintendent.

From among the eight role involvement variables, learning of students had a positive, low-moderate, and significant ($p = .01$) correlation with the respondents' career aspiration to become a superintendent. The single exception was control of resource allocation. Therefore, null hypothesis 7 was rejected.

Finally, the data in Table 6.10 also show a moderate-high, significant, and positive correlation between the assistant superintendents' desired time frame to attain a superintendency and their desire to become a superintendent ($r = .56, p = .001$). Moderate-low, positive, and significant correlations ($p = .001$) were found between their aspiration to become a superintendent and their willingness to relocate to attain a superintendency ($r = .325$) and willingness to travel/commute ($r = .29$).

Predictors of Career Aspirations

As the data in Table 6.11 indicate, using a forward regression model, two variables—their willingness to relocate in order to obtain a superintendency ($p < .000$) and their intended time frame for doing so ($p < .010$)—contributed significantly, explaining 37% of the variance in assistant superintendents' career aspirations to become a superintendent (adjusted R^2 of .353 at p = .000).

CONCLUSIONS

The results of this study indicate that assistant school superintendents are highly satisfied with their work and express a high sense of efficacy in their jobs. Only a modest one-third of the assistant superintendents expressed a desire to become a superintendent, with approximately another third who indicated they might wish to do so. These findings suggest that a conundrum exists when trying to recruit and promote these individuals from the ranks of assistant superintendent to the superintendency.

Those who are highly satisfied with their jobs apparently might be so content with their current role that they do not wish to move away from it. On the other hand, perhaps this satisfaction could entice them to take on the challenges of the superintendency. Related data indicate that the strongest disincentives indicated by the assistant superintendent respondents were family sacrifices and local politics. The data also indicate that those under 49 years

Table 6.10 Correlations between Superintendents' Career Aspiration to Be a Superintendent and Selected Independent and Dependent Variables and Intervening Variables of Role Involvement (N = 159)

Variables	Career Aspiration
Independent Variables	
Age	-.22**
Degree: doctorate	-.03
Recruited to become superintendent	-.21**
Role Involvement	
Interview and select teachers along with principals	.28**
Commit the district to continuous improvement	.34**
Provide access to staff development	.34**
Control resource allocation	-.14
Evaluate principals annually	.32**
Monitor student achievement	.34**
Ensure curricular needs of all students met	.29**
Observe classrooms during school visits	.29**
Set/support goals for student achievement	.32**
Provide leadership of curriculum development	.31**
Report student achievement data to the board	.32**
Dependent Variables	
Job satisfaction	.04
Job efficacy	.18*
Other Career Aspiration Variables	
Desired time frame to attain superintendency	.56**
Willing to relocate to attain a superintendency	.33**
Willing to commute to obtain a superintendency	.29**

* Significant at .05 level (2-tailed). ** Significant at .01 level (2-tailed).

of age and males were more interested in the superintendency than were older assistant superintendents and females.

Table 6.11 Forward Regression Analysis: Variables Best Predicting Assistant Superintendents' Career Aspirations (N = 159)

Variable	B	SE B	Beta	t value	p
Willingness to relocate to obtain superintendent post	.40	.07	.52	6.09	
Intended time frame to obtain superintendent post	.17	.06	.23	2.64	.01

Note: R = .606; R^2 = .367; Adj. R^2 = .353; df = 92; SE = .806; F ratio = 26.088. p = < .000.

Descriptive Analysis of Dependent and Intervening Variables

The results revealed that the vast majority of New York State assistant superintendents in this study expressed satisfaction with their jobs and perceive a strong sense of job efficacy. Overall, they held a very positive perception of their relationship with their superintendent, board of education, and community. Interestingly, while 85% reported that their community strongly supports education, less than half the respondents felt that the community has a good understanding of their role.

With regard to career aspirations, only 27% indicated that they plan to assume the role of superintendent, with 31% remaining undecided. From among these 58% of the respondents, about one-third plan to do so immediately. In one of the few similar statewide studies, Cetorelli (1997) reported that assistant school superintendents in Connecticut were highly satisfied with their jobs; in fact, current job satisfaction was the second most common reason cited as to why they did *not* seek a superintendent post.

Family sacrifices and local politics were the strongest disincentives for those who indicated that they were not planning on becoming a superintendent. Surprisingly, the majority of respondents who are considering becoming superintendents either state no preference or would prefer not to assume the role in their current district. Here are two key recommendations for better preparing and supporting assistant superintendents in their move to the top job in local school districts.

Recommendations

1. *Reorganize the assistant superintendency so that the job functions better to prepare assistant superintendents for the superintendency.* An important finding in this study was that the more specialized groups of assistant superintendents (i.e., personnel, curriculum, business) were less likely to aspire to become superintendents compared to the generalists who hold a wider range of responsibilities. As Whritner (2009) stated,

   Holding the job of assistant superintendent isn't necessarily providing the best on-the-job training required to become an effective CEO. Proficiency at developing curricula and preparing teachers to implement new initiatives is not the same as convincing a school board to spend money on new staff or programs and then grinding through the next mile to convince reluctant community members that a proposed increase in their taxes is worthwhile. (p. 1)

   This study revealed that the generalists' functions seem more similar to the superintendent's, and thus provide the assistant superintendents in this role function with a greater sense of preparedness for the top job.

2. *Be aware of the concerns of Generation X and Y.* An extant review of the literature found that individuals between the ages of 18 and 39 years of age, known as Generation X and Y, place less value on their career advancement and seem to be more family centered than their predecessors (Rogers et al., 2007). Interestingly, this study found a similar trend.

While only 11 respondents were between the ages of 18 and 39, only 4 of them indicated that they will pursue a superintendency. The remaining 7 respondents all strongly agreed or agreed, with "Family sacrifices are important reasons why I do not pursue a superintendency." This finding could hold strong implications for the future superintendent candidate pool.

3. *Shorten the career steps to the assistant superintendency.* This study found that, on average, assistant superintendents have a combined 18 years of teaching and building-level administrative experience prior to becoming an assistant superintendent. Given that 61% of the respondents are 50 years or older and assuming they remain in that position for about 7 years, many prospective superintendent candidates would be nearing retirement age at a time when they would be well prepared for the rigors of the superintendency. The qualified candidate pool could be increased if incumbent assistant superintendents gained relevant experience in a shorter time span.

4. *Give assistant superintendents more opportunities to interact with the community.* Almost half of the respondents agreed or strongly agreed that "The community has a good understanding of my role," which is important for assistant superintendents for several reasons.

First, the role could be in jeopardy in some districts as superintendents and boards of education are confronted with making unprecedented budget cuts during these difficult economic times. Second, aspiring superintendents can benefit from the experience of interacting with the community by, for example, regularly attending parent teacher association (PTA) meetings, school open houses, and other community organization events.

5. *Begin recruiting and supporting assistant superintendents and preparing them to become superintendents before they age out.* Universities, school districts, and boards of education should collaborate to provide support early to aspiring superintendents on how most effectively to reconcile their employment and family life. Consideration should also be given to making changes to the superintendents' position to address the family sacrifices common to the position, such as minimizing the number of late evening meetings and events and eliminating contractual clauses that require superintendents to live within the district.

And districts and superintendent associations should recognize the potential for women in leadership positions as an important source of superintendents from the ranks of assistant superintendents. Gender may matter.

This study explored the assistant school superintendency, specifically focusing on their sense of job satisfaction, job efficacy, and intentions to pursue the superintendency. With the assistant superintendency representing a key pathway to the superintendency, it was important to learn about this group of educational leaders. The assistant superintendent has been neglected in the extant body of research.

The findings of this study may be beneficial to those interested in learning more about the assistant, associate, and deputy superintendents. It also sheds light on the causes of the shrinking pool of superintendent candidates, particularly among the assistants, and offers recommendations that may attract more members of this talented group to pursue the superintendent position.

Even so, this complex problem will not be resolved easily. The study found that the assistant superintendent is not an automatic springboard into the superintendent's job. Changes must be made to address the disincentives associated with the superintendency itself, for men and women leaders, and how to identify and support assistants earlier in their careers—so they are able and willing to assume the top leadership job in public education in a timely, effective way.

REFERENCES

Bandura, A. (1986). *Social foundation of thought and action: A social cognitive theory*. Englewood Cliffs, NJ: Prentice Hall.

Bandura, A. (2006). Guide for constructing self-efficacy scales. In F. Pajares & T. Rudan (Eds.), *Self-efficacy beliefs of adolescents* (pp. 307–337). Greenwich, CT: Information Age Publishing.

Butler, K. (2008). Principal preparation programs. *District Administration, 44*(10), 66–68.

Carlson, R. O. (1962). *Executive succession and organizational change*. Chicago: Midwest Administration Center, University of Chicago, Studies in Educational Administration.

Carlson, R. O. (1972). *School superintendents: Careers and performance*. Columbus, OH: Charles E. Merrill.

Cetorelli, N. D. (1997). *Assistant, deputy, and associate superintendents in Connecticut and their pursuit of superintendency*. Unpublished doctoral dissertation, University of Hartford, CT. Retrieved July 22, 2008, from Dissertations & Theses: Full Text database. (Publication No. AAT 9722324), http://proquest.umi.com/pqdweb?did=739701451&sid=7&Fmt=2&clientId=9148&RQT=309&VName=PQD

Cooper, B. S., & Fusarelli, L. D. (2004). *The promises and perils facing today's school superintendent* (2004). Lanham, MD: Scarecrow Education. Published in cooperation with the American Association of School Administrators.

Crane, S. L. (2006). *A study of job satisfaction of Idaho public school superintendents as compared to job satisfaction of public school superintendents in Hunterdon and Somerset Counties, New Jersey.* Unpublished doctoral dissertation, Idaho State University, Boise. Retrieved July 15, 2008, from ProQuest Digital Dissertations database.

Cranny, C. J., Smith, P. C., & Stone, E. F. (1992). *Job satisfaction: How people feel about their jobs and how it affects their performance.* New York: Lexington Books.

Cuban, L. (1976). *Urban school chiefs under fire.* Chicago: The University of Chicago Press.

Dana, J. A., & Bourisaw, D. M. (2006). *Women in the superintendency: Discarded leadership.* Lanham, MD: Rowman & Littlefield.

Dillman, D. A. (2007). *Mail and Internet surveys: The tailored design method.* New York: John Wiley & Sons.

Dlott, S. (2007). *Surviving and thriving as a superintendent of schools: Leadership lessons from modern American presidents.* Lanham, MD: Rowman & Littlefield Education.

Gall, M. D., Gall, J. P., & Borg, W. R. (2007). *Educational research: An introduction* (8th ed). Boston: Allyn and Bacon.

Galloway, H. (2006). *Barriers faced by women: A study of female superintendents in Texas.* Unpublished doctoral dissertation, Texas State University, San Marcos. Retrieved July 19, 2008, from ProQuest Digital Dissertations database, http://proquest.umi.com/pqdweb?did=1288651831&sid=11&Fmt=2&clientId=9148&RQT=309&VName=PQD

Glass, T. E., & Franceschini, L. (2007). *The state of the American superintendency: A mid-decade study.* Lanham, MD: Rowman & Littlefield.

Grogan, M. (1996). *Voices of women aspiring to the superintendency.* Ithaca, NY: State University of New York Press.

Hayes, W. (2001). *So you want to be a superintendent?* Lanham, MD: Scarecrow Press.

Hodges, B. S. (2005). *Factors influencing qualified candidates' decisions not to pursue the superintendency.* Unpublished doctoral dissertation, University of Northern Colorado, CO. Retrieved July 22, 2008, from Dissertations & Theses: Full Text database (Publication No. AAT 3202452), http://proquest.umi.com/pqdweb?did=1068230131&sid=13&Fmt=2&clientId=9148&RQT=309&VName=PQD.

Kamler, E. (2009). Decade of difference (1995–2005): An examination of the superintendent search consultants' process on Long Island. *Educational Administration Quarterly 45*(1), 115–144.

Latham, G. P., Wexley, K. N., & Pursell, E. D. (1975). Training managers to minimize rating errors in the observation of behavior. *Journal of Applied Psychology, 60*, 550–555.

Locke, E. A. (1976). The nature and consequences of job satisfaction. In M. D. Dunnette (Ed.), *Handbook of industrial and organizational psychologist* (pp. 1297–1349). Chicago: Rand McNally.

Newsmaker: Daniel Domenech. (2008, August). *American School Board Journal*, Retrieved November 30, 2008, from Education Research Complete database, http://search.ebscohost.com.avoserv.library.fordham.edu/login.aspx?direct=true&db=ehh&AN=33065821 &site=ehost–live

Paz, S. (2008, November). Now is the time to recruit future leaders. *District Administration, 44*(12), 73–74. Retrieved November 30, 2008, from Education Research Complete database, http://search.ebscohost.com.avoserv.library.fordham.edu/login.aspx?direct=true&db=ehh &AN=35239611&site=ehost–live

Petersen, G., & Fusarelli, L. (2001, November). *Changing times, changing relationships: An exploration of the relationship between superintendents and boards of education.* Paper presented at the Annual Meeting of the University Council for Educational Administration, Cincinnati, OH.

Rogers, T., Volp, R., Terranova, M., Cattaro, G., Fale, E., Fiore, M. B., Ike, R., Rice, M., Service, R., and Zseller, E. (2007). *Snapshot VI: A study of school superintendents in New York State, 2006.* New York: State Council of School Superintendents.

Simmons, J. C. (2005). Superintendents of color: Perspectives on racial and ethnic diversity and implications for professional preparation and practice. In L. Björk & T. Kowalski (Eds.), *The contemporary superintendent: Preparation, practice and development* (pp. 251–281). Thousand Oaks, CA: Corwin.

Spector, P. E. (1997). *Job satisfaction: Application, assessment, causes, and consequences.* Thousand Oaks, CA: Sage.

Sutton, C. M., Jobe, M. P., McCord, R. S., Jordan, T., & Jordan, K. F. (2008, April). *2007 State of the superintendency mini-survey: Aspiring to the superintendency.* Arlington, VA: American Association of School Administrators, AASA Center for System Leadership. Retrieved August 12, 2008, from www.aasa.org/leadership/content.cfm?ItemNumber =10489.

Waters, J. T., & Marzano, R. J. (2006). *School district leadership that works: The effect of superintendent leadership on student achievement.* Denver, CO: Midcontinent Research for Education and Learning.

Whritner, J. A. (2009, February). Whatever happened to my job description? *School Administrator. 66*(2), 36–37.

Yun, G. W., & Trumbo, C. W. (2000). Comparative response to a survey executed by post, e-mail & web form. *Journal of Computer-Mediated Communication.* Retrieved November 27, 2008, from http://jcmc.indiana.edu/vol6/issue1/yun.html.

Chapter Seven

Superintendent Leadership

George J. Petersen

This chapter examines several professional challenges and potential pitfalls faced by executive school leaders. We provide particular attention to the influence of issues like school reform and accountability, declining enrollment, school governance, and the superintendent–school board relationship. Using these and other professional issues as frameworks, this chapter examines the nature and complexity of district leadership as well as potential professional pitfalls.

Based on the study of 350 California superintendents, we determine the professional learning needs of executive school leaders, concluding with an exploration of some professional development suggestions and ideas designed to enhance the knowledge and skills of superintendents.

AMERICAN SUPERINTENDENTS AND THE EDUCATIONAL EPICENTER

In the last 40 years, state and federal governments have increased the intensity of intervention and scope of control over American schooling, especially during the decades of the 1980s and 1990s, when state and federal governments began a relentless political and rhetorical press for greater "results-based" accountability from our nation's schools (Malen & Cochran, 2008, p. 151).

Also during this time period, local control and influence over the educational outcomes and funding policies of America's schools significantly eroded (Fusarelli & Cooper, 2009; Wirt & Kirst, 2005). Case in point: California developed a comprehensive—and often confusing—mosaic of educational policies, rules, standards, and measures that often bound the hands of local administrators as they sought to make programmatic and financial educational decisions.

State control of educational policy in California has been all encompassing, removing local influence over what is taught, and taking away local authority to determine how much is spent (Picus, 2009). Even with new executive leadership at the federal level, the trend to limit local decision making while increasing levels of public accountability remains a pillar of the educational policy landscape (Parsons, 2010).

In an effort to prod, elbow, or goad schools into compliance, federal and state governments formally endorsed and applied ever-increasing and intrusive sanctions for schools, (e.g., No Child Left Behind Act [Public Law 107-110]). As these reforms persisted and gained momentum in the patois and conscience of American politics, business, and the media, calls for sustainable transformation in American classrooms produced frequent debate, sometimes informed, but always opinionated, regarding the quality of teaching, education, and schooling in the United States.

While some scholars challenged the frenzy about how poorly American students fared when matched against their counterparts in other industrialized nations (Berliner & Biddle, 1995), the constant barrage of negative news regarding public schools became pervasive and was frequently used as a platform for aspiring political officeholders.

Unfortunately, the stories and debate emanating from Washington and state capitals, business roundtables, and the popular news media were more than hyperbole. As the public gaze expanded, queries about the influence and responsibilities of school leaders, specifically principals and district superintendents, became grist for the reform discussion and the subsequent state and federal policies that followed. As a result, speculation and serious questions were raised about the leadership of America's schools and the role school leaders will play in this political mêlée (Petersen & Barnett, 2005).

As one California superintendent commented, "The [federal] government is attempting to insult us into reform" (CA Superintendent, personal communication, April 25, 2007). As politicians, business leaders, and the media thrashed out publicly the level of accountability to be measured out to school leaders, we also began to witness a waning in public trust and confidence once afforded to our schools and their leaders (Carter & Cunningham, 1997).

In an effort to understand the influence of leadership on the school organization and more specifically, the academic achievement of students, scholars began to carefully and systematically investigate the effect that leadership has on instruction and student achievement in an effort to establish a new *center of gravity* (Heck & Hallinger, 1999; Leithwood & Jantzi, 2000a, 2000b; Murphy, 1988; Murphy & Hallinger, 1986; Petersen, 1999).

These empirical investigations of building and district level administrators pointed out that instructionally focused leaders were well-informed political actors who emphasized the importance of an instructional vision, organizational coordination, and socialization of the individuals and groups responsible for teaching and learning. This line of scholarship also indicated the importance of maintaining high levels of visibility, clear communication, and multiple forms of evaluation of instruction. As Petersen and Barnett (2005) pointed out, the move toward instructional leadership and accountability are now critical and anticipated roles of district-level leaders.

Social and Organizational Issues

As local control was steadily replaced by greater federal and state influence on educational outcomes and increased levels of accountability became a central thread in the school reform discussion, other social and political conditions and trends were also actively shaping the texture and complexity of the educational terrain. Social challenges of crushing poverty, marginalized family units, domestic violence, underage pregnancy, drug use, adolescent crime, and incarceration are factors outside of the school's locus of control, but significantly influence student readiness and how schools go about educating and preparing students for life in a fiercely competitive global economy.

The capacity of superintendents to adequately and consistently address these wide-ranging social challenges is compounded by a host of unrelenting professional and organizational variables. Inadequate funding, district size, heightened political activity, declining enrollment, school board–superintendent relationships, and collective bargaining all take their respective toll on superintendents' ability to concentrate on the "results based" goals of current reform efforts (Malen & Cochran, 2008).

Ground Zero

The *American Heritage Dictionary* defines ground zero as *the center of rapid or intense development or change*. The rapidly shifting social, political, and economic trends facing American schools place district superintendents at the epicenter of intense educational change. Pressure of internal and external forces on the professional work of superintendents is not unprecedented. Extant literature has repeatedly demonstrated that as America has changed, the leadership required of superintendents has also undergone significant and rapid transformation in priorities. These shifts, shaped in part by the political and social landscape, are marked by differentiated expectations and demands of an ever-increasingly pluralistic society (Browne-Ferrigno & Glass, 2005; Johnson, 1996).

As Callahan (1964) reminded us, "Sometimes the major thrust for change [of the superintendent's role] has come from outside the profession and sometimes within. Actually, the changes have always been a result of both forces—it is simply a matter of which is strongest in a particular period" (p. 3).

Although uncertainty continues regarding the effects these high-stakes accountability and testing approaches will eventually have on the achievement of students, it is important to keep in mind that these policy streams are very influential in the work of superintendents. Current political, legal, environmental, and organizational conditions require executive school leaders to respond and continuously adjust and readjust to competing demands, and this adaptability is pivotal to their success as well as to the implementation of numerous reform initiatives (Fusarelli & Cooper, 2009).

This chapter provides an overview of some of the unique contexts in which superintendents operate and how the myriad of forces influences efforts to lead school districts. We see that the complexity and intense political nature of many of these daily demands can also lead to potential professional pitfalls. The duress of accountability measures, social issues, and financial policies combine to create a strident and uncertain organizational environment (Johnson & Fauske, 2000) requiring superintendents to rethink and react in different modalities.

This chapter concludes with a discussion of the need for professional development in the lives of these executive leaders. Using a recent study of sitting superintendents, we examine current views regarding professional development and the topics seen as most relevant in their efforts effectively to lead school systems. We conclude with an overview of important characteristics and features of professional development programs for executive school leaders in an effort to assist them in navigating these turbulent waters.

PUBLIC AND ORGANIZATIONAL CHALLENGES

Superintendents routinely find themselves confronting technological, financial, human resource, legal, business, political, and leadership issues. When these problems penetrate the school organization, administrators are expected to confront them. Cuban (1985), reflecting on the superintendent's responsibility in managing the pressures that accompany the vast array of problems, noted that *conflict had indeed become the DNA of the position.*

Even though most experienced leaders are self-aware enough to know that they are not adept at everything (Goldsmith, 2010), individual characteristics such as personality, health, and stress tolerance influence how administrators view and respond to their work (Kowalski, 2006). These dynamics, coupled with the uniqueness of actual work environments for executive school leaders, reflect a wide diversity of students, families, teachers, resources, and communities.

Meeting the demands of external accountability systems and creating dramatic and systemic change in a bureaucratic and institutionalized educational system requires superintendents to engage in political activities, once thought to be antithetical (Kowalski, 2006), and to act in more of a representative and coalition-building manner—similar to actions well known to "politicians" in government (Wirt & Kirst, 2005, p. 169). Although superintendents view themselves as professional educators and not politicians, nearly all adopt political strategies in dealing with board members, staff, the media, and the community at large (Fusarelli, 2005).

As Björk (2005) observed, the push for systemic reform forces superintendents to engage a wide array of community groups and to generate broad-based community support for school improvement initiatives (see also Stanford, 1999). This may be particularly challenging for career-bound (as opposed to place-bound) superintendents who may lack familiarity with the local community (Carlson, 1969). Increasingly diverse communities have multiple centers of power to which superintendents and school boards must attend if they are to engage in systemic reform and school improvement.

Political Pressures and Pitfalls

While managing organizational routines, allocating resources, and making decisions are the *sine qua non* of school leadership, the working and decision-making conditions for superintendents vary and are heavily influenced by such factors as district size, superintendent tenure, board membership, district wealth, and community demographic and support (Glass & Franceschini, 2007). These issues combine to produce an intricate mix of demographic, philosophical, and economic realities and attitudes that often generate conflict as groups vie for influence (Wirt & Kirst, 2005).

Local schools, like all public institutions, are greatly affected by competition among interest groups and can never be divorced from the political realities of a public institution (Kowalski, 2006; Wirt & Kirst, 2005).

A recent statewide investigation queried 350 California school superintendents about the most critical issues facing them.[1] Participants indicated that the top five issues were (1) accountability and improving the academic achievement of students (e.g., NCLB), followed closely by (2) school finance, (3) competing and conflicting demands of the role and community, (4) declining district enrollment, and their (5) work and relationship with the board of education (Petersen, Kelley, Reimer, Mosunich, & Thompson, 2009). These varied responsibilities require engagement of multiple stakeholders, within and external to the district, covering a range of topics and initiatives, often representing distinct and conflicting expectations, political agendas, and educational outcomes.

Practitioners informed us that successful superintendents develop complex skill sets as they encounter these extant issues, individuals, and groups. They must also have highly developed political acumen, communication and public relations skills, knowledge of instructional leadership and evaluation, referent power (influence based on leader identification), and financial expertise. As schools in America evolve, and as the demographics of the students and families that are served by our nation's schools change, considerable challenges await the contemporary superintendent (Petersen et al., 2009).

More importantly, if these tasks are not approached in a systematic, thoughtful, and equitable manner, they can form deep professional chasms, trapping, however well-intentioned, executive school leaders into difficult, precarious, and untenable situations.

To examine the multifaceted nature of issues and the potential pitfalls facing superintendents, we will use three interrelated issues: (1) No Child Left Behind (NCLB), (2) boards of education, and (3) financial policies and declining enrollment, to inform our thinking.

No Child Left Behind

In the last decade, student achievement and closing the achievement gap have become the political *coin-of-the-realm* and powerfully mandated external pressures are the political tool of choice (Petersen & Dlugosh, 2008). The revised Elementary and Secondary Education Act (ESEA), also known as the No Child Left Behind Act of 2001 (NCLB), represents the most comprehensive change to ESEA since its enactment in 1965.

It overrides nearly two centuries of state primacy in K-12 education by requiring that academic performance lead to tangible outcomes for schools—and that children in inadequate school environments have an opportunity to go elsewhere (Hess & Finn, 2004). This expanded federal role has developed into a focal point of education policy and reaches into virtually every public school district, building, and classroom in America. For superintendents this national reform effort represents a sustained shift in thinking in the United States about education and more specifically about administrative roles in American schools (Petersen & Young, 2004).

Taking a cue and lyric from the English rock band The Who, *"meet the new boss, same as the old boss,"* we see that even with a new federal administration, NCLB and high levels of public accountability are not fading into the background. In fact, under President Obama's administration, NCLB policies and expectations are expanding and continue to present notable challenges for superintendents as instructional leaders and resource managers.

Evidently, public education is a political matter, and politicians cannot often wait for slowly developing reform to mature naturally (Hill, Campbell, & Harvey, 2000). In a recent speech to the National Governors Association, President Obama unveiled his intention to increase public school standards in an effort to expand and upgrade NCLB, and requested state governors to form a consortium and develop new and more rigorous reading and math standards.

Past criticism leveled at NCLB has maintained that its provisions let states adopt different standards. As a result, the new plan encourages states to use a common set of college and career-ready standards for use in schools throughout the 50 states. Expectantly, federal monies for schools will be closely linked to the adoption of these new standards (Parsons, 2010).

We also see that other federally and state-supported initiatives, like charter schools, vouchers, and parental choice, provoke substantive questions in the minds of many about the future of public education and those who staff and lead public schools (Kowalski, 2006).

Boards of Education

Advocates of boards of education maintain that lay governance of schools by boards of trustees contributes to the unique strength of democratic decision making in public education by providing a responsive and accessible shared governance system to community stakeholders. Critics on the other hand question their usefulness and/or necessity, provided the current social and political context of systemic reform mandated of schools.

Whether effective or ineffective, school board governance plays a significant role in public education. Board members' tasks in determining the general control and direction of the district, ensuring accountability, establishing processes for the articulation and adoption of policies, and providing community leadership are the building blocks of effective district leadership (Petersen & Fusarelli, 2008).

School boards are dependent upon an array of external, social, economic, and political influences, and their decisions are often predicated upon consideration of a host of factors over which they have little or no control. Boards may not have the information they need to sort through the underlying issues for the scores of complex decisions requiring their approval at each meeting. Quite often they rely on the professional judgment of the superintendent in many educational matters (Boyd, 1976). However, relying on the professional judgment of the superintendent does not equate to unity in decision making.

Björk and Lindle (2001) found that nearly one in five superintendents identified their boards as "fractional," while slightly more than one in ten have "inert" boards (i.e., boards that relegate decision making to the superintendent). This dynamic continues to generate areas of tension in the margin of control and governance of the school district.

Compounding this issue is that a substantial body of research indicates that a district superintendent's success hinges on the relationship that he or she establishes with the board. Since this relationship is pivotal in addressing reform and restructuring efforts, a critical component of success is intricately tied to the ability of the superintendent to influence critical policy decisions made by the board (Fusarelli & Petersen, 2002).

We know now that superintendents exercise considerably more control and influence in the establishment of the board agenda than previously thought (Petersen & Short, 2001); yet formal authority for policy articulation and decision making still resides with the board. Because of this, superintendents must, in most instances, attempt to sway the vote of each individual board member (Boyd, 1976, Blumberg, 1985). Research has also indicated that the willingness of the board to follow the superintendent depends on their acceptance of the superintendent's claim to expertise in specific issue areas and secondarily on board orientation (Greene, 1992).

Financial Policies

The history of American schooling is a story of conflict between two strong traditions. On one side are deeply held beliefs of self-determination, autonomy, and local decision making. These beliefs embrace the idea that parents, teachers, and administrators working in a collaborative fashion are in the best position to meet the educational needs of the local community. On the other side is greater state and federal involvement, some might say, interference, in school policy and decision making. This heightened involvement came about in an effort to address and remedy issues of educational service, equity, and outcomes [e.g., teacher quality and academic standards, categorical programs, and financing] (Kirst, 1989, Hadderman, 1988).

In many states, school finance litigation has mandated the centralization of education funding in an attempt to improve educational adequacy (Hall, 2006). Specifically targeting groups such as students with disabilities, English Learners, and the disadvantaged, federal and state categorical aid programs have been established to address the needs of children and families previously overlooked. As these policies came into play, local entities lost a significant amount of autonomy and influence. Declining enrollment, voter resistance to increase property taxes, coupled with court decisions concerning student rights and due process, further eroded local control (Hadderman, 1988; Picus, 2009).

This centralization of educational policy and decision making was a reversal of traditional American political ideology, which rejected distant government in favor of localized management (Hadderman, 1988). Although a body of research indicates that centralized funding policies attempt to achieve greater social equity through finance reform, the loss of local autonomy irritates many superintendents, and evidence suggests that the most significant improvements occur when individual schools are given greater autonomy, not less (Kirst, 1989).

As a result of these internal and external forces, the discretionary zone of local superintendents and boards has been gradually constricted into a smaller area (Wirt & Kirst, 2005). The superintendent's discretion is squeezed from the top by increasing regulations from legislative, administrative, and judicial arms of the federal and state governments.

In addition, the influence of external private interest groups and professional reformers (e.g., the Broad Foundation, the Carnegie Corporation, the Bill and Melinda Gates Foundation, the Kauffman Foundation, and the Wallace Readers Digest Funds, etc.,) has expanded along with interstate groups such as the Education Commission of the States and nationally oriented organizations such as the Council for Exceptional Children. All over the nation, networks of individuals and groups sprang up to spread school finance reform, competency testing, increased academic standards, and other programs (Wirt & Kirst, 2005, p. 51).

Declining Enrollment

Compounding the erosion of local fiscal discretionary authority is the problem of declining enrollment. Organizations like the American Association of School Administrators (AASA) have examined the impact of declining enrollment on a national level for several years. Declining enrollments are a product of significant demographic shifts that may be linked to economic conditions (e.g., land/resource changes and housing costs) and welfare reform (French & Thomas, 2002; Jimerson, 2006). A loss of students translates into a loss of per-pupil state revenue.

As a result, some districts are unable to fully engage in reform initiatives intended to enhance teaching capacity and increase student achievement. When the enrollment decline is chronic, it generates serious financial distress because of the loss of revenue. This financial hemorrhage usually results in deep cuts in programs, staff, and resources. Small rural schools are especially vulnerable to these problems, since they have proportionally less leeway in finding cost-saving areas. Eventually, declining enrollment can lead to their closure in spite of their value to rural communities and students.

In a report for the California County Superintendents Educational Services Association (CCSESA), French and Thomas (2002) reported numerous problems for district leaders as the result of declining enrollment. Examples included (a) high rates of governing board member turnover, (b) a loss of local control in the sense that community members did not want to serve on the board, (c) an inability to recruit and retain qualified staff, and (d) high rates of administrator turnover. The authors then stated, "The net effect is a degree of district paralysis with respect to long-term planning, standards-based quality control, and overall effectiveness" (p. 2). The state's weak economy and a flat K-12 state enrollment projection for the next several years also exacerbate the issue and place superintendents in untenable situations (Tyler & Kibby, 2004).

Strategies to deal with declining enrollments deployed by executive leaders have varied, but most have entailed efforts to cultivate inclusive decision-making environments so that stakeholders would have opportunities to bring their "collective wisdom" to school improvement efforts. Scholars writing about democratic decision making have emphasized the importance of respecting different points of view (Fusarelli, Kowalski, & Petersen, in press) and varied group interests (Mawhinney, 2001).

In light of declining enrollments, dwindling resources, and heightened accountability, pressures on superintendents to move toward democratic leadership styles have mounted. The affected administrators find themselves in a complex web of political, social, and economic expectations—competing perspectives that reflect an array of organizational and community priorities affecting the type and scope of issues that are addressed.

It is evident that in response to societal, political, and economic pressures for change, there seems to be an ever-increasing expectation for a more transparent and inclusive leadership orientation of district leaders. These pressures, coupled with a shifting landscape of American schooling, require new ways of thinking about the ongoing work and development of district superintendents. For superintendents to succeed, they will need to recruit and involve the support of multiple stakeholders to increase their influence in decision making at the local and state levels.

Strategies that enable district leaders to acquire the professional dexterity to address the politics and political power configurations of communities, policy makers, and board members are vital in their efforts to lead reform and to be the *guardians* of public education (Glass, Björk, & Brunner, 2000).

THE NEED FOR PROFESSIONAL LEARNING AND DEVELOPMENT

Political and social complexities inherent in seeking effective solutions to the multifaceted problems facing schools require superintendents to generate coherency among the assorted political and social systems, while simultaneously managing the competing agendas directed at the policies, practices, and outcomes of schools. The type of leadership required to transform teaching and learning that move students beyond basic skills to proficient and advanced levels, as well as ensuring that all teachers are knowledgeable and competent in supporting students' success, is significantly more challenging than making sure students are in their desks with a certified teacher assigned to each room (Young, 2005).

Executive leaders are under immense pressure to focus on immediate test score gains versus continuous improvement in teaching and learning. Coupled with limited resources, this pressure hinders leaders' ability to maintain focus and ensure that all students are able to fulfill individual, family, and community aspirations; spur economic growth; and advance democracy (Darling-Hammond, 2007).

What Superintendents Say They Need

In an effort to understand more fully the professional development needs of superintendents, we solicited the perspectives of California superintendents regarding professional topics and issues they believe would assist them in roles as executive leaders (previously described). Based on pilot interviews as well as the extant literature (Glass & Franceschini, 2007; Kowalski, 2006), nine areas of professional development were presented to 350 district leaders who were instructed to rank professional development topics they felt would increase their leadership abilities and effectiveness.

The top five areas were (1) budgeting, (2) systemic thinking and reform, (3) strategic planning, (4) policy and politics, and (5) public relations and communications with instruction, assessment and data management of subgroups tying for fifth (Petersen et al., 2009).

Interestingly, superintendents ranked systemic thinking and reform and budget as the top two areas in which they desired further training to be effective leaders. However, we might have assumed, given the public scrutiny of NCLB, they would have selected instructional practices for improving the academic achievement of students. Research has shown that in some instances, district leaders, particularly as it pertains to the core technology of curriculum and instruction, will delegate their responsibilities to other personnel as they focus the majority of their time on the other administrative functions of the district (Bredeson, 1996).

In general, what the other three areas (e.g., strategic planning, policy and politics, and public relations) reveal are superintendents' recognition of and need for highly developed interpersonal communication skills to carry out their responsibilities as district leaders (Petersen et al., 2009).

Enriching Professional Capacity

A variety of national, state, and private organizations regularly schedule conferences, seminars, workshops, and content-specific meetings designed to provide education professionals with the very best and most up-to-date training and information about particular topics in education. Albeit that many of these agencies and groups espouse the effectiveness of their programs, research has demonstrated that the extent to which leadership competencies are acquired and professional practice enhanced depends on a variety of factors (Berg & Barnett, 1998).

Kent Peterson (2002) outlined empirically established characteristics and recommendations for the professional development of school principals. While a number of aspects are specific to the professional development needs of building level leaders, several of the components may be applied to district or executive level leaders. For example:

- Professional development should be structured to enhance learning and knowledge of current technologies and best practices;
- Professional development should be career staged with learning opportunities designed around the tenure and experience of the leader. Programs should be designed specifically for aspiring, novice, or experienced administrators;
- Programs should have a clear focus and strong culture-building aspects;
- The core mission of programs should focus on leading schools that promote high-quality learning for all students;
- The curriculum should be carefully designed and sequenced with attention to prior experience and learning;
- Programs should provide a set of intensive experiences over a period of time, combining multiday retreats and partial-day experiences;
- The curriculum should be varied, engaging, and use the most current and effective approaches for helping administrators learn their craft;
- Topics being addressed should provide core skills and knowledge that will enhance leadership as well as professional skills related to specific administrative procedures, contractual requirements, and community characteristics of the district.

These recommendations are consistent with related research focused on enhancing the learning of school leaders, particularly the importance of culture building and mentorship aspects of professional development. In a cross-national study of superintendents from the United States and Sweden, Bredeson, Klar, and Johansson (2009) found that executive leaders indicated that learning opportunities, involving interactions with peer groups in collaborative learning environments, were the most enriching and beneficial in enhancing their professional learning and competencies.

As the authors reported, "Given the fragmented and informal nature of most professional development for superintendents and the interdependence between superintendents' work, and their professional learning, it is not surprising that these leaders described the importance of interacting with their peers and tapping into the expertise and insights of other people" (2009, p. 145).

CONCLUSION

As executive leaders encounter complex issues, collaborate with diverse and competing groups of stakeholders, build coalitions, manage conflict, lead school reform, and model good judgment, the opportunities for success or the pitfalls of failure depend on their tacit knowledge, experience, and skill sets. The sheer number and variety of professional tasks require a fundamental shift in thinking about the role and responsibilities of district superintendents and their ability to adapt and change in a turbulent organizational environment.

Certainly, successful executive leaders are able to blend professional knowledge, politics, expertise, and practice in their efforts to lead schools. Yet the ability to successfully integrate all of the components is not guaranteed upon assuming the helm. Both research and practice make it clear that the ability to enhance the leadership capacity of district superintendents is through ongoing professional development. Career-staged, collaboratively designed learning opportunities are acknowledged as effective and meaningful forms of professional development.

In these types of settings and experiences, superintendents engage in discussions and activities that reinforce best practices and expand their thinking and knowledge around relevant, contemporary, and often pressing professional issues.

If our schools and students are to achieve higher standards of performance, then our leaders must be supported in their efforts to become more skilled at their craft. Superintendents are the key linchpins in the reform of schools, and their reputation and survival are largely dependent on their ability to integrate and employ an array of professional skills and attributes. A body of research suggests that for professional development programs to be effective, they must have strong theoretical and research based curriculum designed to provide authentic experiences in collegial settings over extended periods of time. Through these types of programs, executive leaders are able to cultivate experience, competencies, skills, and professional ethos that will renew and retain them in their positions as they work to improve American schools and remain their guardians.

NOTE

1. The experience levels of participating superintendents ranged from 1 year (10%) to 15 years (15%), with 49.5% serving from 3 to 10 years in the role. Gender of these district leaders was 36.8% females and 63.2% males.

REFERENCES

Berg, J., & Barnett, B. (1998, April). *The school district superintendent: Attention must be paid*. Paper presented at the annual meeting of the American Educational Research Association, San Diego, CA.

Berliner, D. C., & Biddle, B. J. (1995). *The manufactured crisis: Myths, fraud and the attack on America's public schools*. Reading, MA: Addison-Wesley Publishing Company.

Björk, L. G. (2005). Superintendent-board relations: An historical overview of the dynamics of change and sources of conflict and collaboration. In G. J. Petersen & L. D. Fusarelli (Eds.), *The politics of leadership: Superintendents and school boards in changing times* (pp. 1–22). Greenwich, CT: Information Age Publishing.

Björk, L. G., & Lindle, J. C. (2001). Superintendents and interest groups. *Educational Policy, 15*(1): 76–91.

Blumberg, A. (1985). A superintendent must read the board's invisible job description. *American School Board Journal, 172*(9), 44–45.

Boyd, W. L. (1976). The public, the professionals, and educational policy: Who governs? *Teachers College Record, 77*(4), 539–578.

Bredeson, P. V. (1996). Superintendents' roles in curriculum development and instructional leadership: Instructional visionaries, collaborators, supporters, and delegators. *Journal of School Leadership, 6*(3), 243–264.

Bredeson, P. V., Klar, H. W., & Johansson, O. (2009, Spring). Superintendents as collaborative learners in communities of practice: A socio-cultural perspective on professional learning. *Journal of School Public Relations, 30*(2), 128–149.

Browne-Ferrigno, T., & Glass, T. E. (2005). Superintendent as organizational manager. In L. G. Björk & T. J. Kowalski (Eds.), *The contemporary superintendent: Preparation, practice and development* (pp. 137–161). Thousands Oaks, CA. Corwin Press.

Callahan, R. E. (1964). The superintendent of schools: A historical analysis. Final report of Project S-212. Washington, D.C.: U.S. Office of Education, Department of Health, Education, and Welfare.

Carlson, R. O. (1969). Career and place bound school superintendents: Some psychological differences. A project report. Eugene, OR: Eugene Center for Advanced Study of Educational Administration.

Carter, G. R., & Cunningham, W. G. (1997). *The American school superintendent: Leading in an age of pressure.* San Francisco: Jossey-Bass.

Cuban, L. (1985). Conflict and leadership in the superintendency. *Phi Delta Kappan, 67*(1), 28–30.

Darling-Hammond, L. (2007). The flat earth and education: How America's commitment to equity will determine our future. *Educational Research, 36*(6), 318–334.

French, J., & Thomas, G. (2002). *Declining enrollment in California (Report of the Declining Enrollment Work Group, California County Superintendents Educational Services Association).* Updated Fall 2002. Retrieved February 15, 2010, from wwwstatic.kern.org/gems/ccsesaAtWork/DecliningEnrollmentpaper3.pdf

Fusarelli, B. C., & Cooper, B. S. (2009). *The rising state: How state power is transforming our nation's schools.* Albany, NY: SUNY Press.

Fusarelli, L. D. (2005). Future research directions and policy implications for superintendent-school board relationships. In G. J. Petersen & L. D. Fusarelli (Eds.), *The politics of leadership: Superintendents and school boards in changing times* (pp. 181–197). Greenwich, CT: Information Age Publishing.

Fusarelli, L. D., Kowalski, T. J., & Petersen, G. J. (in press). Promoting civic, "public" engagement in education through distributive leadership and deliberative democracy. *The Journal of Leadership and Policy in Schools.*

Fusarelli, L., & Petersen, G. J. (2002). Changing times, changing relationships: An exploration of current trends influencing the relationship between superintendents and boards of education. In G. Perreault & F. C. Lunenburg (Eds.), *NCPEA 2002 Yearbook: The Changing World of School Administration* (pp. 282–293). Lanham, MD: Scarecrow Press.

Glass, T. E., Björk, L., & Brunner, C. (2000). *The study of the American school superintendency.* Arlington, VA: American Association of School Administrators.

Glass, T. E., & Franceschini, L. A. (2007). *The state of the American school superintendency: A mid-decade study.* Lanham, MD: Rowman & Littlefield Education.

Goldsmith, M. (2010, February 19). *The mark of a great leader.* Message posted to http://blogs.hbr.org/goldsmith/2010/02/the_mark_of_a_great_leader.html. Harvard Business Review.

Greene, K. R., (1992). Models of school board policy making. *Educational Administration Quarterly, 28*(2): 220–236.

Ground zero. (2010). *In The American Heritage® Dictionary of the English Language, 4th Ed.*, Retrieved February 9, 2010, from http://dictionary.reference.com/browse/ground%20zero.

Hadderman, M. L., (1988). *State vs. local control of schools. ERIC Digest Series Number 24*. ERIC Educational Reports. Retrieved March 2, 2010, from http://findarticles.com/p/articles/mi_pric/is_198800/ai_3830717127/.

Hall, J. (2006). The dilemma of school finance reform. *Journal of Social, Political and Economic Studies, 31*(3): 175–190.

Heck, R., & Hallinger, P. (1999) Conceptual models, methodology, and methods for studying school leadership. In J. Murphy & K. Seashore Louis (Eds.), *The 2nd handbook of research in educational administration* (pp. 141–162). San Francisco, CA: McCutchan.

Hess, F. M., & Finn, C. E. (2004). *Leaving no child behind? Options for kids in failing schools*. New York: Palgrave.

Hill, P. T., Campbell, C., & Harvey, J. (2000). *It takes a city: Getting serious about urban school reform*. Washington, D.C.: Brookings Institution Press.

Holloway, J. H. (2001, February). Setting standards for the school superintendent. *Educational Leadership, (58)*5, 84–85.

Jimerson, L. (2006, February). *Breaking the fall: Cushioning the impact of rural declining enrollment*. The Rural School and Community Trust. Retrieved February 27, 2010, from www.ruraledu.org.

Johnson, S. M. (1996). *Leading to change: The challenge of the new superintendency*. San Francisco: Jossey-Bass.

Johnson, B. L., Jr. & Fauske, J. R. (2000), Principals and the political economy of environmental enactment. *Educational Administration Quarterly*, Vol. 36, No. 2, 159–185.

Kirst, M. (1989, Spring). Who should control our schools? *California School Boards Journal, 47*(4), 38–47.

Kirst, M. (2004). Turning points: A history of American school governance. In N. Epseing (Ed.), *Who's in charge here? The tangled web of school governance and politics* (pp.14–41). Denver, CO: Education Commission of the States.

Kowalski, T. J. (2006). *The school superintendent: Theory, practice, and cases (2nd Ed.)*. Thousand Oaks, CA: Sage.

Kowalski, T. J., Petersen, G. J., & Fusarelli, L. D. (2007). *Effective communication for school administrators: A necessity in an information age*. Landham, MD: Rowman & Littlefield.

Leithwood, K., & Jantzi, D. (2000a). Principal and teacher leadership effects: A replication. *School Leadership & Management, 20*(4), 415–434.

Leithwood, K., & Jantzi, D. (2000b). The effects of transformation leadership on student engagement with school. *Journal of Educational Administration, 38*(2), 112–129.

Malen, B., & Cochran, M. V. (2008). Beyond pluralistic patterns of power: Research on the micropolitics of schools. In B. S. Cooper, J. G. Cibulka, & L. D. Fusarelli (Eds.), *Handbook of education politics and policy* (pp. 148–178). New York: Routledge.

Mawhinney, H. (2001). Theoretical approaches to understanding interest groups. *Educational Policy, 15*(1), 187–214.

Maze, J. G. (2009, August). Superintendent perceptions of their professional development in leadership for student achievement at Texas regional education service centers. A paper presented at the *National Council of Professors of Educational Administration*. San Antonio, TX.

Murphy, J. (1988). The instructional leadership role of the school principal: An analysis. *Educational Evaluation and Policy Analysis, 10*(2), 71–79.

Murphy, J. (2002, April). Reculturing the profession of educational leadership: New blueprints. *Educational Administration Quarterly, 38*(2), 176–191.

Murphy, J., & Hallinger, P. (1986). The superintendent as instructional leader. Findings from effective school districts. *Journal of Educational Administration, 24*(2), 213–236.

Parsons, C. (2010, February 22). Obama to announce new effort to improve No Child Left Behind. *Los Angeles Times*. Retrieved February 29, 2010, from www.latimes.com/news/nation-and-world/la-na-obama-education22-2010feb22,0,954399.story.

Petersen, G. J. (1999, May). Demonstrated actions of instructional leaders: A case study of five superintendents. *Education Policy Analysis Archives, 7*(18). Retrieved February 19, 2010, from http://epaa.asu.edu/ojs/article/view/553

Petersen, G. J., & Barnett, B. G. (2005). The superintendent as instructional leader: Current practice, future conceptualizations and implications for preparation. In L. G. Björk & T. J. Kowalski (Eds.), *The contemporary superintendent: Preparation, practice and development* (pp. 107–136). Thousand Oaks, CA. Corwin Press.

Petersen, G. J., & Dlugosh, L. (2008). How NCLB has affected the practice of school district superintendents. In T. J. Kowalski & T. J. Lasley (Eds.), *Handbook of data-based decision-making for education* (pp. 455–470). London: Taylor and Francis Publishers.

Petersen, G. J., & Fusarelli, L. D. (2008). Systemic leadership amidst turbulence: Superintendent-school board relations under pressure. In T. Alsbury (Ed.), *The future of school board governance: Relevancy and revelation* (pp. 115–136). Lanham, MD: Rowman & Littlefield.

Petersen, G. J., & Fusarelli, L. D. (Eds.). (2005). *The politics of leadership: Superintendents and school boards in changing times*. Greenwich, CT: Information Age Publishing (IAP).

Petersen, G. J., Kelly, V., Reimer, C., Mosunich, D., & Thompson, D. (2009, Fall). An investigation of district leaders' perceptions of forces that complicate efforts to succeed. *Journal of School Public Relations, 30*(4), 281–308.

Petersen, G. J., Sayre, C., & Kelly, V. (2007). What teachers think: An investigation of teachers' perceptions regarding the superintendent's influence on instruction and learning. *California Instructional Leadership Forum, Vol. 2*, pp. 1–29.

Petersen, G. J., & Short, P. M. (2001, October). The school board president's perception of the district superintendent: Applying the lens of social influence and social style. *Educational Administration Quarterly, 37*(4), 533–570.

Petersen, G. J., & Young, M. D. (2004, July). The No Child Left Behind act and its influence on current and future district leaders. *The Journal of Law and Education, 33*(4), 343–363.

Peterson, K. (2002, April). The professional development of principals: Innovations and opportunities. *Educational Administration Quarterly, 38*(2), 213–232.

Picus, L. O. (2009). California. In B. C Fusarelli, & B. S. Cooper (Eds.). *The rising state: How state power is transforming our nation's schools* (pp. 14–42). Albany: SUNY Press.

Sergiovanni, T. J., Kelleher, P., McCarthy, M. M., Wirt, F. M. (2004). *Governance and administration* (5th Ed.). Boston: Pearson Education, Inc.

Stanford, J. (1999). *Victory in our schools*. New York: Bantam Books.

Tyler, C. E., & Kibby, R. W. (2004, May-June). Small districts, sharp axes. *Leadership Magazine. The Association of California School Administrators*. Retrieved February 27, 2010, from www.findarticles.com/p/articles/mi_m0HUL/is_5_33/ai_n6149362

Wirt, F. M., & Kirst, M. W. (2005). *The political dynamics of American education* (3rd ed.). Richmond, CA: McCutchan Publishing Corp.

Young, M. D. (2005). Building effective school system leadership: Rethinking preparation and policy. In G. J. Petersen & L. D. Fusarelli (Eds.), *The politics of leadership: Superintendents and school boards in changing times* (pp. 157–179). Greenwich, CT: Information Age Publishing.

Young, M. D., Petersen, G. J., & Short, P. M. (2002, April). The complexity of substantive reform: A call for interdependence among key stakeholders. *Educational Administration Quarterly, 38*(2), 137–176.

Epilogue: Thoughts for the Future

Naftaly S. Glasman and
Lynnette D. Glasman

In addressing the significant challenges before us, we need to rethink (and possibly redefine) school leadership and school governance. To date, we have only tiptoed around the edges of these sensitive issues. (McCarthy, 2002, p. 216)

TIPTOEING

Why rethink? Why redefine? What has changed that necessitates the rethinking and redefining? The key to successful educational leadership was identified in the early 1950s as striking a healthy balance between not abandoning the organizational goals and continuing to care for the organizational workers ("goal orientation and consideration"). Was it not similar, beginning in the 1990s, when educational leaders were impressed with the "human relations" approach to leadership and organization? This approach's fundamental assumption was the need to establish a give-and-take relationship between employees and the organization.

I would argue that what has changed in educational leadership over the last two decades has been the demands for educational accountability. In the early 1990s it was still only rhetoric. In the new century it reached as far as high-stakes student testing. Gradually, outcome-based leadership has become leaders' accountability for the schools.

Clearly that change does require rethinking. The reason for these new ideas is that without identifying exactly who in the school is accountable to whom, for what, and with what consequences, then leaders' accountability could very well become an empty concept. And since accountability is a highly sensitive issue, I would guess that when McCarthy writes that we have only tiptoed around the edges of these sensitive issues, she includes accountability among them. In this epilogue I wish to suggest that during this period when the country's economy is in a downturn, accountability is THE major issue facing school leaders. But first I wish to show how Conley and Cooper's volume in fact leads the reader to this very conclusion.

EXAMINING IN DEPTH

This book offers several selections that can be grouped into three sequentially ordered themes: issues associated with training for the job, personal aspirations while on the job, and matching the job with its contexts. Three studies make up "the preparation and adjustment" part. Orr and Pounder consider policies and research reviews as key inputs to designing high-quality programs.

The authors examine select school outcome criteria that result from program quality. They find that accessibility and scheduling are among the many factors that enhance student self-assessed acquired knowledge. Trainees report that an intensive internship experience affects trainees' career intentions and actual career advancements.

The next two studies continue to identify specific and extremely useful sets of realities that educational leaders of tomorrow need to become aware of, better understand, and even work on in order to hone their previously established leadership skills. Marinell concentrates on the teacher workforce and offers examples of midcareer science and mathematics teachers with engineering and other backgrounds outside of education. Socialization is seen as being important here.

Trachtman and Cooper revisit the educational leaders' role of mentoring their faculty in the "art and science" (my term) of teaching. Their working assumption: principals of tomorrow must quickly grow into "master teachers." They show what these activities involve and outline the accrued benefits.

The book continues with an occupation about the personal future of the educational leader. I see this occupation as a positive consideration, one of which might be reflecting a commitment to a career in education. Bauer and Brazer are concerned with issues of self-efficacy among new school principals. Their study examines how and to what extent a leader's role ambiguity and related variables account, at least in part, for a sense of isolation that ultimately might bring up doubts about one's sense of self-efficacy. Will what I do really make a difference? might be one concern.

Leach and Cooper's study reports on the role of assistant superintendents. These are experienced educational leaders. Here, too, the authors explore the leaders' job satisfaction as possibly affecting efficacy that, in turn, might affect the leaders' future career aspirations. "Am I good enough to advance?" might be a relevant question here.

Petersen looks at highly ranked educational executives (superintendents). He assumes that incumbents who reach this top rank would already be satisfied with their leadership role. But no! Petersen finds that these leaders see their role as designed to bring about change. And in order to accomplish this goal, they feel the need to learn more than what they currently know. They need to acquire "an appropriate professional capability to enhance change."

This latter section of the book deals with organizational and social contexts within which school leaders work. This topic is of utmost importance, in my opinion. I am taking the liberty to report here that with the help of my students, I have studied leaders' definitions of leadership right at the beginning of their work on the job and then again a month later. The first and the second sets of definitions turned out to be substantially different from each other in most cases. An analysis of the definitions led to the speculation that knowing more about the job context was the key reason for the change in definition. In this way, one can view the second definitions as signs of professional growth in the career life cycle.

LEADERS' SELF-ACCOUNTABILITY

The challenge that educational leaders face in responding to demands for accountability will never go away. It is always either present or about to appear. In fact, that challenge typically appears when the society wants schools to correct its own ills. I offer a working redefinition of educational leadership that is strongly related to accountability trends. It is offered to the educational leaders of tomorrow that they may use it as a base and amend as needed. Let me begin with this definition: Leaders move simultaneously ahead of and alongside followers.

In this definition, the word *moving* implies continuous change. "Moving ahead of followers" implies learning about and attempting to understand the organizational and social contexts of schooling that are in constant flux.

On the other hand, "moving alongside followers" implies learning about—and attempting to understand—the educational wishes of the schools' immediate stakeholders, which might also be in constant flux. At the same time I integrate my visions with the realities associated with (1) my teachers who serve as models of diversity, (2) my curriculum that reflects discovery grounded in past and present knowledge and skills, and (3) the students, parents, administrators, and support personnel who are my full partners in executing the schooling process.

Finally, the term "practicing self-accountability" is used to denote nothing less than being answerable to oneself for one's actions and facing the consequences resulting from those actions. Self-accountability must be the cornerstone of all leadership attributes and all leadership behaviors.

Before attempting to "teach self-accountability" to others, we need to practice it and become proficient at it. In comfortable economic, social, and political times, we could learn self-accountability from anyone, including our followers. But learning self-accountability is not as simply accomplished in periods of difficulty and uncertainty.

BARRIERS AND HOPE

Difficulty and uncertainty create barriers for leaders to effectively teach self-accountability. No one knows when or how the society will overcome these difficulties and still come out intact. Tomorrow's educational leaders might find the practice of self-accountability problematic to pursue and not necessarily for a lack of ethical attributes.

Bolman and Deal's (2008) conceptual framework of leadership styles remains useful as a guide to leadership behavior today, even while tremendous shortages of funding for education exist. Consider, for example, fiscal constraints that cause a principal to make the decision to assign a physical education teacher to teach two periods of mathematics or history. Bolman and Deal's framework would encourage the principal to sort through not only work design issues but also how new job definitions affect teachers' needs (structural and human resource frames).

Bolman and Deal (2008) offer two additional leadership guides: the "Political" and the "Symbolic" Leadership styles. Bista and Glasman (1998a, 1998b) found that educational leaders do not readily admit to practicing these two leadership styles. Practicing and teaching self-accountability using these styles must be at the core of educational leadership. Employing them effectively could very well serve to restore faith in the educational system and its potential to serve individuals and the society. To match self-accountability with this book's messages has been my undertaking in this epilogue.

The book is about preparing the best educational leaders throughout the life cycle. I would suggest that those responsible for creating and meeting these three challenges must themselves practice self-accountability:

1. Practicing self-accountability in *preparing and recruiting* the best leaders is to select those with strengths to meet existing and projected needs.

2. *Sustaining* the best leaders through self-accountability is to provide them with quality support such as in analyzing situations or backing up decisions before even considering adding resources, and
3. *Retaining* the best leaders requires helping them to become self-accountable and efficacious stakeholders in their work. And our children, our nation, and our world can truly benefit from getting and keeping the best school leaders, a major task of our schools and universities.

REFERENCES

Bista, M. B., & Glasman, N. S. (1998a). Principals' perceptions of their approaches to organizational leadership: Revisiting Bolman and Deal. *Journal of School Leadership, 8*(1), 28–48.

Bista, M. B., & Glasman, N. S. (1998b). Principals' approaches to leadership: Their antecedents and student outcomes. *Journal of School Leadership, 8*(2), 109–136.

Bolman, L. G., & Deal, T. E. (2008). *Reframing organizations: Artistry, choice and leadership.* San Francisco: Jossey-Bass.

McCarthy, M. M. (2002). Educational leadership preparation programs: A glimpse at the past with an eye toward the future. *Leadership and Policy in Schools*, Glasman, N. S. (Guest Editor) *1*(1), 201–221.

About the Contributors

Sharon Conley, Ph.D., is professor of education in the Gevirtz Graduate School of Education at University of California, Santa Barbara. Her latest articles include "Organizational Routines in Flux: A Case Study of Change in Recording and Monitoring Student Attendance" with Ernestine K. Enomoto in *Education and Urban Society* and "Teacher Role Stress, Satisfaction, Commitment and Intentions to Leave: A Structural Model" in *Psychological Reports*.

Bruce S. Cooper, Ph.D., is professor of educational leadership and policy at Fordham University Graduate School of Education in New York City. His latest books as editor and author include *Handbook on Education Politics and Policy* with James Cibulka and Lance Fusarelli and *The Rising State: How State Power Is Transforming Our Nation's Schools* with Bonnie Fusarelli. He is former president of the Politics of Education Association and a recent recipient of the Jay D. Scribner Award for Mentoring from the University Council of Education Administration.

Scott C. Bauer, Ph.D., is associate professor in the Education Leadership Program at George Mason University in Fairfax, Virginia.

S. David Brazer, Ph.D., is associate professor and program coordinator in the Education Leadership Program at George Mason University in Fairfax, Virginia.

Lynette D. Glasman, Ph.D., is a former program evaluator in various school districts in California.

Naftaly S. Glasman, Ph.D., is research professor of education in the Department of Education at the University of California, Santa Barbara.

David F. Leach, Ed.D., is a principal in the Ramapo Central School District in Suffern, New York. He also serves as an adjunct professor of education at Long Island University.

William H. Marinell, Ed.D., is research associate in the Research Alliance for New York City Schools at New York University in New York City.

Margaret Terry Orr, Ph.D., is associate professor in the Educational Leadership Department at Bank Street College of Education in New York City.

George J. Petersen, Ph.D., is dean and professor in the School of Education at California Lutheran University in Thousand Oaks, California.

Diana G. Pounder, Ph.D., is dean and professor in the College of Education at University of Central Arkansas in Conway, Arkansas.

Roberta Trachtman, Ed.D., is director of teaching and learning at New Visions for Public Schools in New York City.

www.ingramcontent.com/pod-product-compliance
Lightning Source LLC
Chambersburg PA
CBHW021851300426
44115CB00005B/111